Mani Singh Basi is a barrister and a specialist in family law disputes relating to children, particularly those with an international dimension. He regularly appears in complicated cases in the High Court and Court of Appeal. Mani was the winner of the 2024 Legal Personality of the Year award, the 2024 Legal Aid Barrister of the Year award, the 2023 Family Law Junior Barrister of the Year award and 2022 Family Law Commentator of the Year award.

A Practical Guide to the Participation of Children in Family Law Proceedings

A Practical Guide to the Participation of Children in Family Law Proceedings

Mani Singh Basi

Law Brief Publishing

Published 2024 by Law Brief Publishing, an imprint of Law Brief Publishing Ltd
30 The Parks
Minehead
Somerset
TA24 8BT

www.lawbriefpublishing.com

Paperback: 978-1-916698-41-3

PREFACE

This book will provide a practical overview to enable practitioners working within the family law system to properly address the issue of children participation in family law proceedings. In particular, this book will consider the various ways in which children can directly or indirectly participate in family law proceedings and the necessity of such participation in light of recent case law developments. Further, the book will also consider the duties that lawyers and other professionals have when it comes to children participation.

In the book, there will be chapters considering children participation across the following areas of the law: private law disputes, public law matters, cases concerning child abduction and the inherent jurisdiction of the High Court. Further, the book will consider a number of topical issues relating to the scope and necessity of welfare reports in different areas of family law, the involvement of the local authority in undertaking assessments, the issue of separate representation, children meeting the judge, the role of guardians as well as an overview of the current family procedure rules, legislation and case law.

This book will consider a number of practical issues that practitioners are often faced with when managing cases and when dealing with evidential issues concerning children. The book will assist practitioners in enabling them to best present their case from the outset of proceedings, all the way to the end of the case, across all the relevant areas of family law. The book specifically considers public, private and international (Hague and non-Hague) proceedings.

The law is correct as of 1st June 2024.

Mani Singh Basi
June 2024

CONTENTS

CHAPTER ONE

AN INTRODUCTION TO CHILDREN PARTICIPATION

Introduction to chapter

This Chapter will provide an overview of the topics that this book will consider. In particular, it will set out why it is important for practitioners to think at the outset and during the whole course of the proceedings as to children participation in proceedings. In this book, reference will be made to 'children' but of course proceedings can also concern 'a child' only. Equally, at times, reference may be made to 'child' but the context can also be provided for in relation to 'children'.

Children Participation – An Introduction

Disputes relating to children are vast ranging and the severity of the issues involved can vary a tremendous amount. As this book will consider, different principles apply in terms of the law whether proceedings are classified as private law or public law proceedings. The outcomes of such proceedings can also vary in terms of its severity, with for example public law proceedings resulting in placement orders and children being adopted. In both proceedings, children can be involved in many different ways. Further, the role of children in other family law proceedings is also different, for example in child abduction proceedings. Child abduction proceedings can be split into two forms, firstly the inherent jurisdiction and secondly child abduction pursuant to the 1980 Hague Convention. Both areas of child abduction have resulted in a lot of appellant cases emphasising and establishing the importance of children participation.

There continues to be even at the time of writing this book (March 2024) studies and work undertaken to assess and understand the mechanism in which children are heard in family law proceedings[1].

In certain circumstances children can be separately represented, either instructing a solicitor directly or having their interests preserved by a guardian appointed on their behalf (the latter being is automatic in public law proceedings). This is a Chapter within itself.

Further, whilst the majority of the law that will be considered in this book can be found in the form of statute such as the Children Act 1989 or treaties such as the 1980 Hague Convention, the vast majority of guidance appears through case law and the Family Procedure Rules 2010 ['FPR']. Both the FPR and case law has considered the tricky issues in existence in trying to find the right balance in ensuring children are heard in proceedings which ultimately deal with them directly. The law is however clear – the child's welfare is paramount, the child's wishes and feelings appear in the welfare checklist and more importantly, the child's voice should and must be heard. However, the mechanism in which the child's voice can be heard is what can vary case-by-case depending upon a number of different factors.

It is a well-recognised common feature of domestic and international Convention jurisprudence that the voice of a subject child will need to be heard. For example, Article 12 UNCRC requires that to ensure participation of children in proceedings affecting them requires that measures taken must be '*...to be effective and meaningful, it needs to be understood as a process, not as an individual one-off event.*'[2]. These rights of children are to be applied in accordance with one of the core principles of the UNCRC, the concept of *evolving capacity* under Article 5 of the

1 The Nuffield Foundation completed a sample study which included 40,753 family law cases that started in 2019/2020.

2 Committee on the Rights of the Child General Comment No 12 (2009): The Right of the Child to be heard CRC/C/GC/12

UNCRC which extends to '*...to processes of maturation and learning whereby children progressively acquire knowledge, competencies and understanding, including acquiring understanding about their rights and about how they can best be realized...*'.

These aims through Article 12 were emphasised by Baroness Hale in In Re D (A Child) (Abduction: Rights of Custody)[3] when she referred to Article 11(2) of Brussels IIa as enunciating a principle of "universal application" and to this being "consistent with our international obligations under article 12" of the UNCRC.

In General Comment No.12 (2009) The right of the child to be heard, the Committee said:

> *"25. The realization of the right of the child to express her or his views requires that the child be informed about the matters, options and possible decisions to be taken and their consequences by those who are responsible for hearing the child, and by the child's parents or guardian. The child must also be informed about the conditions under which she or he will be asked to express her or his views. This right to information is essential, because it is the precondition of the child's clarified decisions."*
>
> ...
>
> *(ii) "Either directly, or through a representative or an appropriate body"*
>
> *35. After the child has decided to be heard, he or she will have to decide how to be heard: "either directly, or through a representative or appropriate body". The Committee*

[3] [2006] UKHL 51, paragraph 58

recommends that, wherever possible, the child must be given the opportunity to be directly heard in any proceedings.

36. The representative can be the parent(s), a lawyer, or another person (inter alia, a social worker). However, it must be stressed that in many cases (civil, penal or administrative), there are risks of a conflict of interest between the child and their most obvious representative (parent(s)). If the hearing of the child is undertaken through a representative, it is of utmost importance that the child's views are transmitted correctly to the decision maker by the representative. The method chosen should be determined by the child (or by the appropriate authority as necessary) according to her or his particular situation. Representatives must have sufficient knowledge and understanding of the various aspects of the decision- making process and experience in working with children.

37. The representative must be aware that she or he represents exclusively the interests of the child and not the interests of other persons (parent(s)), institutions or bodies (e.g. residential home, administration or society). Codes of conduct should be developed for representatives who are appointed to represent the child's views." (emphasis added).

Turning to the concept of legal representation, which is also an essential feature of domestic law and rights in England and Wales, in General Comment No. 14 (2013) on the right of the child to have his or her best interests taken as a primary consideration (art. 3, para. 1) the Committee said:

"e) Legal representation

96. The child will need appropriate legal representation when his or her best interests are to be formally assessed and determined by courts and equivalent bodies.. In particular, in cases where a child is referred to an administrative or judicial procedure

> *involving the determination of his or her best interests, he or she should be provided with a legal representative, in addition to a guardian or representative of his or her views, when there is a potential conflict between the parties in the decision."* [emphasis added]

In England and Wales, the domestic law has developed over the years to recognise the growing and essential weight that must be attached to the voice of children, after all – proceedings relate to them. There are a number of different systems and ways in which children can effectively participate in these proceedings. This may be through welfare reports where children can express their views, through organisations such as Cafcass, or a local authority or independent social worker. At times, a guardian can be appointed for children, or a child may instruct a solicitor directly. A child can meet the trial judge, or write a letter to the judge. The situation and the developing feature of the various ways that children can participate was summarised in Mabon v Mabon[4] [2005] Thorpe LJ at paragraph 25, where the following was stated:

> ".. In our system we have traditionally adopted the tandem model for the representation of children who are parties to family proceedings, whether public or private. First the court appoints a guardian ad litem who will almost invariably have a social work qualification and very wide experience of family proceedings. He then instructs a specialist family solicitor who, in turn, usually instructs a specialist family barrister. This is a Rolls Royce model and is the envy of many other jurisdictions. However its overall approach is essentially paternalistic. The guardian's first priority is to advocate the welfare of the child he represents. His second priority is to put before the court the child's wishes and feelings. Those

4 [2005] EWCA CIV 634

> priorities can in some cases conflict. In extreme cases the conflict is unmanageable. ...".

Conclusion of Chapter

Therefore, as this book will outline from this introduction – the role of children in private, public and international disputes are sometimes similar, but also different. There are various ways, enshrined by procedure rules, legislation (both domestic and international) and case law which outlines the importance of active children representation.

CHAPTER TWO

PRIVATE LAW CHILDREN DISPUTES: CHILDREN PARTICIPATION

Introduction

This Chapter will consider the issue of children participate in private law children disputes. In particular, this Chapter will consider the concept of 'welfare reports' and the circumstances in which a local authority can be involved in private law proceedings.

Private Law – What is it?

Private law disputes are those proceedings where there is a dispute as to the use of parental responsibility or any other conflict in respect of the upbringing of the child which requires the courts determination. Proceedings can be varied in terms of complexity and the issues that the court is required to consider. At times, proceedings can escalate where the proceedings may turn into public law proceedings or there are fact-finding hearings. Private law disputes are commenced and heard in the Family Court but can be allocated to either Lay Justices, District Judges or Circuit Judges. In certain circumstances, cases can be reallocated to the High Court in cases of particular complexity.

Proceedings concerning children in the private law context is governed by the Children Act 1989. The ambit is stipulated by Section 1 (1) which states:

> '(1) When a court determines any question with respect to—
>
> (a) the upbringing of a child; or
>
> (b) the administration of a child's property or the application of any income arising from it,
>
> the child's welfare shall be the court's paramount consideration.
>
> (2) In any proceedings in which any question with respect to the upbringing of a child arises, the court shall have regard to the general principle that any delay in determining the question is likely to prejudice the welfare of the child.'

The statute then refers to the 'welfare checklist'. It goes on to record:

> '(3) In the circumstances mentioned in subsection (4), a court shall have regard in particular to—
>
> (a) the ascertainable wishes and feelings of the child concerned (considered in the light of his age and understanding);
>
> (b) his physical, emotional and educational needs;
>
> (c) the likely effect on him of any change in his circumstances;
>
> (d) his age, sex, background and any characteristics of his which the court considers relevant;
>
> (e) any harm which he has suffered or is at risk of suffering;

(f) how capable each of his parents, and any other person in relation to whom the court considers the question to be relevant, is of meeting his needs;

(g) the range of powers available to the court under this Act in the proceedings in question.

(4) The circumstances are that—

(a) the court is considering whether to make, vary or discharge a section 8 order, and the making, variation or discharge of the order is opposed by any party to the proceedings; or

(b) the court is considering whether to make, vary or discharge a special guardianship order or an order under Part IV.

(5) Where a court is considering whether or not to make one or more orders under this Act with respect to a child, it shall not make the order or any of the orders unless it considers that doing so would be better for the child than making no order at all.'

In the private law context, there are other provisions relating to the Children Act 1989 on topics such as parental responsibility, who can apply for orders and other provisions. However, as for the purposes of considering children participation, the welfare checklist is an important starting point.

Applying the Welfare Checklist

As can be seen from the welfare checklist above, there is a series of factors the court must consider when concerned with a dispute. Ultimately, it is the court who is considering the checklist and applying it to the facts of a case, and this is an important consideration that people need to be aware off working in this field, it is the court's application and decision. However, the court often is required to be assisted in their decision-making process.

In the run up to the Children Act 1989, the Law Commission[5] proposed the checklist and set out the aims of the provision:

'Perhaps most important of all, we are told that such a list could assist both parents and children in endeavouring to understand how judicial decisions are made. At present, there is a tendency for advisers and clients (and possibly even courts) to rely on "rules of thumb" as to what the court is likely to think best in any given circumstances. A checklist would make it clear to all what, as a minimum would be considered by the court.'

However, given there are many different factors within the checklist, the question of weight to be attached to each one has been subject to case law debate. Ultimately, 'each case turns on its own facts and the weight to be given to various factors will change from case to case'[6].

---

5 Family Law Review of Child Law: Guardianship and Custody (1988) Law Com No 172

6 *Re W (Children) (Relocation: Removal Outside the Jurisdiction)* [2011] EWCA Civ 345 per Wall P at [117].

Welfare Reports

The first step to consider welfare in proceedings is often the Section 7 report. When proceedings commence via a c100, the process enters into a gatekeeping stage. From this moment, Cafcass will be tasked to embark upon safeguarding checks. The remit and purpose of safeguarding letters appears in PD12B, Rule 13.1 onwards which states:

> **'13.1**
>
> Where an application is made for a child arrangements order (but not necessarily for specific issue or prohibited steps orders), before the FHDRA (see paragraph 14 below) Cafcass / CAFCASS Cymru shall identify any safety issues by the steps outlined below.
>
> 13.2
>
> Such steps shall be confined to matters of safety. The Cafcass Officer or (in Wales) the Welsh Family Proceedings Officer (WFPO) shall not discuss with either party before the FHDRA any matter other than one which relates to safety. The parties will not be invited to talk about other issues, for example relating to the substance of applications or replies or about issues concerning matters of welfare or the prospects of resolution. If such issues are raised by either party, they will be advised that such matters will be deferred to the FHDRA when there is equality between the parties and full discussion can take place which will be a time when any safety issues that have been identified can also be taken into account.

13.3

In order to inform the court of possible risks of harm to the child Cafcass / CAFCASS Cymru will carry out safeguarding enquiries. For all child arrangements orders this will include seeking information from local authorities, and carrying out police checks on the parties. For all other applications received from the court on the form C100, Cafcass / CAFCASS Cymru will carry out a screening process and will undertake those checks if in the professional judgment of the Cafcass officer, or the WFPO in Wales, such checks are necessary.

13.4

Cafcass / CAFCASS Cymru will, if possible, undertake telephone risk identification interviews with the parties and if risks of harm are identified, may invite parties to meet separately with the Cafcass Officer, or WFPO in Wales, before the FHDRA to clarify any safety issue.

13.5

Cafcass / CAFCASS Cymru shall record and outline any safety issues for the court, in the form of a Safeguarding letter (in Wales, this is called a 'Safeguarding report').

13.6

The Cafcass officer, or WFPO, will not initiate contact with the child prior to the FHDRA. If contacted by a child, discussions relating to the issues in the case will be postponed to the day of the hearing or after when the Cafcass officer or WFPO will have more knowledge of the issues.

> **13.7**
>
> Within 17 working days of receipt by Cafcass / CAFCASS Cymru of the application, and at least 3 working days before the hearing, the Cafcass Officer or WFPO shall report to the court, in a Safeguarding letter / report, the outcome of the risk identification work which has been undertaken. The letter / report should specify which court forms filed by the parties (C100, C7 and C1A) have been considered.
>
> **13.8**
>
> Further, Cafcass and CAFCASS Cymru are required, under section 16A Children Act 1989, to undertake (and to provide to the court) risk assessments where an officer of the Service ('Cafcass Officer' or WFPO) suspects that a child is at risk of harm'

The safeguarding letter is essential in cases involving risk and domestic abuse. However, the safeguarding letter highlights other important information:

- Police involvement;
- Previous local authority involvement; and
- Recommendations for the case, including case management.

The above is important because it may be apparent that there are historic social work involvement relating to a family. If so, then a social work local authority may be better placed to deal with the case than perhaps Cafcass.

Ultimately, the first piece of advice to look out for in the safeguarding letter is whether a Section 7 is recommended and if so, on what remit and what timescales. The Section 7 report will go through the welfare checklist and be an intensive piece of work where the reporting officer will provide the court with recommendations at the Dispute Resolution Appointment hearing ['DRA'] in the hope parties can settle the case.

The Section 7 report is also the gateway to consider further involvement in respect of children. A child subject to the report has the opportunity through the report to provide their wishes and feelings and the reporting officer will consider their welfare when providing recommendations. However, the Section 7 report may also provide other direct ways to involve children. Typically, they may involve:

- A letter to the court written by the children which goes towards the wishes and feelings aspect of the welfare checklist; and / or

- A recommendation that a guardian should be appointed and the reasons for outlining why.

The child subject to the report can prepare a letter, which is often attached to or incorporated in the report and such a letter is under their wishes and feelings category. Alternatively, the officer may recommend that the child is joined to proceedings / have a guardian appointed for them when that applies.

It is worth noting that it does not only have to be Cafcass who is to do a Section 7 report. The benefit of course with Cafcass is that if a guardian is appointed, it would be somebody from Cafcass and they have their own internal systems in place and procedures. However, as outlined earlier there can be cases where there have been previous or existing social work involvement. In these circumstances, Cafcass will, and it will have to be Cafcass given they are the only ones that can do the safeguarding letter, recommend from the outset in the safeguarding letter that the local authority is likely to be best placed to embark upon the Section 7 report. This could be not only due to the existing or past local authority involvement, but also the child subject to the proceedings may be part of a child in need or child protection plan and ultimately, there may be an allocated social worker in existence. Another option is an independent social worker to complete a Section 7 report which is sometimes an option where reports are sought much quicker. For example, in relocation cases where there may be an element of urgency or if the parties are able to afford an expert, it is likely an independent social worker can prepare a report much quicker, sometimes 6 – 8 weeks, or even less, in comparison to some areas where Cafcass can take in excess to 16 weeks at times.

Appointing a guardian

A guardian serves as 'both the voice of the child and eyes and ears of the court': R. (R., E., J. and K.) v. CAFCASS[7] at paragraph 38 per Munby LJ and Thirlwall J. The appointment of a guardian is an important feature of all areas of the law relating to children. However, often we see a guardian appointed in private law children disputes, and they are often referred to as a '16.4 guardian'. Accordingly, it will be reviewed within this Chapter.

The starting point is to consider PD16 FPR 2010. Rule 7.1 sets out the task and important points the court must consider:

> '7.1
>
> Making the child a party to the proceedings is a step that will be taken only in cases which involve an issue of significant difficulty and consequently will occur in only a minority of cases. Before taking the decision to make the child a party, consideration should be given to whether an alternative route might be preferable, such as asking an officer of the Service or a Welsh family proceedings officer to carry out

[7] [2011] EWHC 1774 (Admin)

> further work or by making a referral to social services or, possibly, by obtaining expert evidence'.

There is therefore the language of 'only a minority of cases' being specified. The rules go on to state from 7.2:

> 'The decision to make the child a party will always be exclusively that of the court, made in the light of the facts and circumstances of the particular case. The following are offered, solely by way of guidance, as circumstances which may justify the making of such an order –
>
> (a) where an officer of the Service or Welsh family proceedings officer has notified the court that in the opinion of that officer the child should be made a party;
>
> (b) where the child has a standpoint or interest which is inconsistent with or incapable of being represented by any of the adult parties;
>
> (c) where there is an intractable dispute over residence or contact, including where all contact has ceased, or where there is irrational but implacable hostility to contact or where the child may be suffering harm associated with the contact dispute;
>
> (d) where the views and wishes of the child cannot be adequately met by a report to the court;
>
> (e) where an older child is opposing a proposed course of action;
>
> (f) where there are complex medical or mental health issues to be determined or there are other unusually complex issues that necessitate separate representation of the child;

(g) where there are international complications outside child abduction, in particular where it may be necessary for there to be discussions with overseas authorities or a foreign court;

(h) where there are serious allegations of physical, sexual or other abuse in relation to the child or there are allegations of domestic abuse not capable of being resolved with the help of an officer of the Service or Welsh family proceedings officer;

(i) where the proceedings concern more than one child and the welfare of the children is in conflict or one child is in a particularly disadvantaged position;

(j) where there is a contested issue about scientific testing'.

There is therefore a clear checklist of factors the court has to consider. Often, Cafcass at their initial safeguarding letter may note the particular complexity or factors, to suggest that a guardian may be necessary, or they should look into it further at a later stage, for example if a fact-finding hearing is directed, the issue may be revisited post such a hearing.

In practice, often given the importance of risk pursuant to PD12J and assessing disputed facts where fact-finding hearings are deemed necessary, a guardian is more often than not specifically considered post-fact finding hearing. This is because, where there is a fact-finding hearing, the issue of welfare reports, further assessments and risk management, is considered thereafter. On the basis of factually determined points, a guardian may be necessary to proceedings. This does however need to be considered in line with rule 7.4 which states:

'7.4

When a child is made a party and a children's guardian is to be appointed –

(a) consideration should first be given to appointing an officer of the Service or Welsh family proceedings officer. Before appointing an officer, the court will cause preliminary enquiries to be made of Cafcass or CAFCASS CYMRU. For the relevant procedure, reference should be made to the practice note issued by Cafcass in June 2006 and any modifications of that practice note.

(b) If Cafcass or CAFCASS CYMRU is unable to provide a children's guardian without delay, or if for some other reason the appointment of an officer of the Service of Welsh family proceedings officer is not appropriate, rule 16.24 makes further provision for the appointment of a children's guardian.'

Appointing a guardian can however, at whatever stage of private law proceedings create a delay. This is specifically recognised in PD16, where it is stated at paragraph 7.3:

'7.3

It must be recognised that separate representation of the child may result in a delay in the resolution of the proceedings. When deciding whether to direct that a child be made a party, the court will take into account the risk of delay or other facts adverse to the welfare of the child. The court's primary consideration will be the best interests of the child'.

Practitioners must therefore have regard to the above point and the necessity to balance and argue either for or against, the risk of delay against the welfare of the child.

Guardian being appointed

If a guardian is appointed, then the participation of the child to the proceedings arguably becomes greater. The guardian will appoint a solicitor, and their position shall be advanced during the course of proceedings. This is far greater than a Section 7 report in isolation which at times, may only involve a single visit between the reporter and the children, and may or may not involve consideration of supervision of contact which is to inform the report.

Upon a guardian being appointed, again Practice Direction 16 sets out the duties:

> 7.6
>
> It is the duty of a children's guardian fairly and competently to conduct proceedings on behalf of the child. The children's guardian must have no interest in the proceedings adverse to that of the child and all steps and decisions the children's guardian takes in the proceedings must be taken for the benefit of the child.
>
> 7.7
>
> A children's guardian who is an officer of the Service or a Welsh family proceedings officer has, in addition, the duties set out in Part 3 of this Practice Direction and must exercise those duties as set out in that Part.'

For ultimate clarity, as reference is made to Part 3, which provides much more information, it sets out the following:

'How the children's guardian exercises duties – investigations and appointment of solicitor

6.1

The children's guardian must make such investigations as are necessary to carry out the children's guardian's duties and must, in particular –

(a) contact or seek to interview such persons as the children's guardian thinks appropriate or as the court directs; and

(b) obtain such professional assistance as is available which the children's guardian thinks appropriate or which the court directs be obtained.

6.2

The children's guardian must –

(a) appoint a solicitor for the child unless a solicitor has already been appointed;

(b) give such advice to the child as is appropriate having regard to that child's understanding; and

(c) where appropriate instruct the solicitor representing the child on all matters relevant to the interests of the child arising in the course of proceedings, including possibilities for appeal.

6.3

Where the children's guardian is authorised in the terms mentioned by and in accordance with section 15(1) of the Criminal Justice and Court Services Act 2000 or section 37(1) of the Children Act 2004 (right of officer of the Service or Welsh family proceedings officer to conduct litigation or exercise a right of audience), paragraph 6.2(a) will not apply if the children's guardian intends to have conduct of the proceedings on behalf of the child unless –

(a) the child wishes to instruct a solicitor direct; and

(b) the children's guardian or the court considers that the child is of sufficient understanding to do so.

6.4

Where rule 16.21 (Where the child instructs a solicitor or conducts proceedings on the child's own behalf) applies, the duties set out in paragraph 6.2(a) and (c) do not apply.

How the children's guardian exercises duties – attendance at court, advice to the court and reports

6.5

The children's guardian or the solicitor appointed under section 41(3) of the 1989 Act or in accordance with paragraph 6.2(a) must attend all directions hearings unless the court directs otherwise.

6.6

The children's guardian must advise the court on the following matters –

(a) whether the child is of sufficient understanding for any purpose including the child's refusal to submit to a medical or psychiatric examination or other assessment that the court has the power to require, direct or order;

(b) the wishes of the child in respect of any matter relevant to the proceedings including that child's attendance at court;

(c) the appropriate forum for the proceedings;

(d) the appropriate timing of the proceedings or any part of them;

(e) the options available to it in respect of the child and the suitability of each such option including what order should be made in determining the application; and

(f) any other matter on which the court seeks advice or on which the children's guardian considers that the court should be informed.

6.7

The advice given under paragraph 6.6 may, subject to any direction of the court, be given orally or in writing. If the advice is given orally, a note of it must be taken by the court or the court officer.

6.8

The children's guardian must –

(a) unless the court directs otherwise, file a written report advising on the interests of the child in accordance with the timetable set by the court; and

(b) in proceedings to which Part 14 applies, where practicable, notify any person the joining of whom as a party to those proceedings would be likely, in the opinion of the children's guardian, to safeguard the interests of the child, of the court's power to join that person as a party under rule 14.3 and must inform the court –

(i) of any notification;

(ii) of anyone whom the children's guardian attempted to notify under this paragraph but was unable to contact; and

(iii) of anyone whom the children's guardian believes may wish to be joined to the proceedings.

(Part 18 sets out the procedure for making an application to be joined as a party in proceedings.)

How the children's guardian exercises duties – service of documents and inspection of records

6.9

The children's guardian must serve and accept service of documents on behalf of the child in accordance with rule 6.31 and, where the child has not himself been served and has sufficient understanding, advise the child of the contents of any document so served.

6.10

Where the children's guardian inspects records of the kinds referred to in –

(a) section 42 of the 1989 Act (right to have access to local authority records); or

(b) section 103 of the 2002 Act (right to have access to adoption agency records)

the children's guardian must bring all records and documents which may, in the opinion of the children's guardian, assist in the proper determination of the proceedings to the attention of –

(i) the court; and

(ii) unless the court directs otherwise, the other parties to the proceedings.

How the children's guardian exercises duties – communication of a court's decision to the child

6.11

The children's guardian must ensure that, in relation to a decision made by the court in the proceedings –

(a) if the children's guardian considers it appropriate to the age and understanding of the child, the child is notified of that decision; and

(b) if the child is notified of the decision, it is explained to the child in a manner appropriate to that child's age and understanding.'

Therefore the duty of a guardian is wide-ranging and comprehensive, and is a key feature in ensure a child subject to proceedings can properly participate and outline their experiences / views where necessary in accordance with their welfare.

Older Children Participation

The definition of a child and whether an order should encompass a child of a particular age is always an area of contention. In private law disputes, proceedings relating to a 15 year-old for example may raise the question as to the no order principle, or whether it is in the child's interests for private law proceedings to continue and or be considered in light of the age and the degree and strength of wishes and feelings.

The point is emphasised in Re C (Older Children: Relocation)[8] (Rev 1) [, in a private law context Jackson J (as he then was) held as follows:

> *"A further and central element of the situation is that the children of this family are in fact young persons, being boys now aged 17 and 15. The case illustrates the particular caution that should be felt by any court seeking to make arrangements for children of this age. In the first place, it is likely to be inappropriate and even futile to make orders that conflict with the wishes of an older child. As was memorably said in Hewer v Bryant [1970] 1 QB 357 in a passage approved in Gillick v West Norfolk and Wisbech Area Health Authority [1986] 1 AC 112: "... the legal right of a parent to the custody of a child ends at the eighteenth birthday and even up till then, it is a dwindling right which the courts will hesitate to enforce against the wishes of the child, the older he is. It starts with a right of control and ends with little more than advice." Nowadays, the 'no order' principle goes even further and requires the court to justify making any order at all, regardless of whether it is in support of the child's wishes or in opposition to them. With an older child, the court's grasp cannot exceed its reach, any more than a parent's can, and attempts to regulate something that is beyond effective regulation can only create a forum for*

---

8 [2015] EWCA CIV 1298

> *disagreement and distract the family from solving its own problems."*

Conclusion of Chapter

As this chapter outlines, there are various ways children can participate in private law proceedings. There are overlaps on other areas such as public and international disputes, which will be considered in later chapters. However, in summary, the key consideration is the concept of 'welfare reports'. They have to be determined as appropriate at the first hearing, the FHDRA and it is the first way in which children can actively participate in proceedings. Notwithstanding this, during the course of proceedings matters can get more complicated. In these circumstances, it may be a guardian is appointed on behalf of a child. The rules, duties, expectations and requirements are all set out in the Family Procedure Rules.

CHAPTER THREE

PUBLIC LAW PROCEEDINGS AND CHILDREN PARTICIPATION

Introduction

This Chapter will consider the children's participation in public law proceedings. Public law proceedings are referred to proceedings where there is state involvement, FOR EXAMPLE a local authority issuing proceedings for a care or supervision order. Proceedings often deal with very serious allegations. As this chapter will outline, a guardian is appointed immediately in such proceedings to ensure a child's interests is advanced throughout the duration of the case. This is vitally important in public law proceedings in particular where a child could be made subject to a placement order and ultimately placed for adoption.

A number of considerations in the private law chapter equally apply to this public law chapter. There are of course, very different considerations due to the different issues that can arise in public law proceedings, but the role of the guardian is extremely similar. There are not however, 'welfare reports' like in private law children disputes. However, there are 'final analysis' which is evidence on behalf of the guardian at the end of the proceedings, after the local authority and respondents have responded to the final care plan.

Guardians in Public Law Proceedings

As outlined in the private law chapter, the concept of appointing a guardian on behalf of the child appears in public law proceedings. Automatically, when a local authority is applying for a public law order, a child shall be joined to the proceedings and a guardian shall be appointed.

The history in relation to this is key. The Court of Appeal judgment in In *R (R and Others (Minors)) v CAFCASS*[9] provides useful history. In the judgment, it was outlined from paragraph 4 – 10:

> *'The children's guardian: background*
>
> 4. *The need for a court making decisions about whether or not a child requires the protection of a care order to have advice from a social worker who is independent of the applicant local authority was given prominence in the report into the death of Maria Colwell in 1974 and was reemphasised in subsequent reports into the deaths of Jasmine Beckford (1985), Heidi Koseda (1986) and Kimberley Carlile (1987). Whilst statute law was slow to deliver a requirement for the appointment of an independent social worker to represent the interests of a child in statutory care proceedings under the Children and Young Persons Act 1969, many of the more complicated child care cases were in fact brought before the court outside the statutory scheme by using wardship proceedings and it was the norm in wardship cases for the child to be represented by a guardian ad litem, often the Official Solicitor, who could instruct an independent social worker to advise the court and would*

[9] [2012] EWCA Civ 853

provide legal representation to advocate the recommendations of that advice before the court.

5. *The Children Act l989 [CA 1989], which came into force on 14th October 1991, expanded the statutory scheme so that it now encompasses all cases where local authorities seek to take a child into care on the basis that the child is suffering, or is likely to suffer significant harm. In consequence of CA 1989, s 100, wardship is no longer available for this purpose. The 1989 Act, drawing upon the recommendations from the past enquiries into child death and the favourable experience of the wardship court, established a statutory requirement for the appointment of a guardian ad litem and a solicitor for the child in every child care case unless the court is satisfied that it is not necessary to do so in order to safeguard the child's interests (CA 1989 s 41 (1)). It is very rare for the court in care proceedings to dispense with the appointment of a solicitor and guardian and this "tandem model" of these two different professionals both acting to represent the interests of the individual child in a care case has been the norm for the past twenty years.*

6. *The original title given to the independent social work role, "guardian ad litem", was changed in 2001 to "children's guardian" by the Criminal Justice and Court Services Act 2000, s 74, and the relevant court rules.*

7. *The availability of the tandem model in child care proceedings has been under focus in the recent review of the Family Justice System carried out for the government by a panel chaired by Mr David Norgrove. In its interim report (March 2011) at paragraph 4.243 onward the Norgrove panel reported as follows:*

   "The tandem model is fundamental to our system and receives strong support....the court needs an impartial social

work opinion even though this results in a degree of duplication with the role of the Local Authority social worker."

8. *In its final report (November 2011) the panel reported respondents expressing "strong support for the tandem model". The panel recommended to the government that the tandem model should be retained, but that the pressure of high caseloads and limited resources should be reflected in a proportionate deployment of the solicitor and children's guardian either working together or individually as the needs of a particular case require.*

9. *In its formal response to the Norgrove Review (February 2012) the government accepted the recommendation that the tandem model should be retained with resources carefully prioritised and allocated. The response states (page 63):*

   "the government agrees that the tandem model remains an important vehicle for ensuring that children's wishes, needs and feelings can be understood and independently represented within the court."

10. *Following that brief description of the history, role and value of a children's guardian in care proceedings, it is now necessary to turn to the relevant statutory provisions'*

Turning to the statutory provisions, care proceedings are governed by the general provisions in CA 1989, Part I (ss 1–7) and those relating to 'care and supervision' in Part IV (ss 31-42):

CA 1989, s 41 establishes a duty on the court to appoint 'an officer of the Service' (in England a CAFCASS officer, or in Wales an officer of CAFCASS Cymru) to act a children's guardian in 'specified proceedings', which definition includes care proceedings:

'(1) For the purpose of any specified proceedings, the court shall appoint an officer of the Service ... for the child concerned unless satisfied that it is not necessary to do so in order to safeguard his interests.

(2) The officer of the Service ... shall –

(a) be appointed in accordance with rules of court; and

(b) be under a duty to safeguard the interests of the child in the manner prescribed by such rules.

(3) Where –

(a) the child concerned is not represented by a solicitor; and

(b) any of the conditions mentioned in subsection (4) is satisfied,

the court may appoint a solicitor to represent him.

(4) The conditions are that –

(a) no officer of the Service ... has been appointed for the child;

(b) the child has sufficient understanding to instruct a solicitor and wishes to do so;

(c) it appears to the court that it would be in the child's best interests for him to be represented by a solicitor.

(5) Any solicitor appointed under or by virtue of this section shall be appointed, and shall represent the child, in accordance with rules of court.

(6) In this section "specified proceedings" means any proceedings –

(a) on an application for a care order or supervision order;

...

(10) Rules of court may make provision as to –

(a) the assistance which any officer of the Service ... may be required by the court to give to it; ...'

As further outlined in Re R at paragraph 15:

'CA 1989, s 42 gives extensive powers to the children's guardian to investigate relevant local authority records. In addition the rules of court establish further powers and duties attaching to the appointed children's guardian in order for the officer to be able to discharge their primary duties of acting for the child in the proceedings and safeguarding the child's interests'

Termination of a Guardian

In certain circumstances, the termination of the guardian has entered the court arena. It was comprehensively dealt with by MacDonald J in QS v RS and T (by her Children's Guardian)[10] In the case of N (A Child) (Termination of children's guardian)[11] [HHJ Carter sitting in the Family

10 [2016] EWCH 1443 (Fam)

11 [2022] EWFC B16

Court in Birmingham summarised the legal principles and outlined the following, taken from MacDonald J, at paragraph 45 of the judgment:

> 'a) *As the terminology used in the test in Porter v McGill suggests, the question of apparent bias is ordinarily considered in the context of the conduct of a person or persons occupying a judicial or quasi-judicial role. Where the person whose conduct is in question is not acting in a judicial or quasi-judicial capacity it is inappropriate for the case to be approached in the same way as one would approach a person performing a normal judicial role or quasi-judicial role; a situation where the person is making a determination (R v Secretary of State for Trade and others ex parte Perestrello and another [1981] 1 QB 19 at 35). In such circumstances, the position of the person whose conduct is the subject of criticism is better considered by reference to whether the person in question was under a duty to act fairly, the ambit of that duty, and whether they have acted with the requisite degree of fairness, rather than by reference to the concept of apparent bias (R v Secretary of State for Trade and others ex parte Perestrello and another [1981] 1 QB 19 at 34). I pause to note that, pursuant to FPR 2010 r 16.27(1)(b) and PD 16A para 7.6, a children's guardian appointed pursuant to FPR 2010 r 16.4 is required to conduct the proceedings on behalf of the child fairly.*
>
> b) *Art 6 of the ECHR enshrines the right to a fair hearing. When considering whether a hearing has been fair, the court will look at the proceedings as a whole as well as any alleged individual deficiencies (Barberá, Messegué and Jarbado v Spain (1988) 11 EHRR 360 at [68]). The right to a fair trial guaranteed by Art 6 is not confined to the 'purely judicial' part of the proceedings. Unfairness at any stage of the litigation process may involve a breach of Art 6 (Re L (Care: Assessment: Fair Trial) [2002] 2 FLR 730).*

c) *Where it is said that biased or unfair conduct on the part of person under a duty to advise the court will lead to bias or unfairness in the proceedings, such a causal link must be demonstrated. In R v Gough [1993] AC 646 at 664C the House of Lords held that it must be shown that by reason of the adviser participating in the decision making process there is a real likelihood that he or she would impose his or her influence on the tribunal (see also R (Royal Brompton and Harefield NHS Foundation Trust) v Joint Committee of Primary Care Trusts and Another [2012] EWCA Civ 472 at [132]).*

[18. Paragraph 18 details the provisions of FPR 2010 r 16.4.]

19. Within this context, it is important to note the observations of Macur LJ in MW v Hertfordshire County Council [2014] EWCA Civ 405 (a case in which the children's guardian was appointed pursuant to FPR 2010 r 16.3) at [21] and [32] respectively that the children's guardian is not a "neutral" party or participant in proceedings and that the children's guardian does not have a "special" status within proceedings. Whilst the children's guardian is required to proffer advice to the court, in doing so the guardian becomes a witness subject to the same judicial scrutiny as any other witness. The children's guardian starts with no special advantage in proceedings as compared with other witnesses.

20. When the court is reaching its decision with respect to the welfare of a child it must consider all the evidence in the case including, but not limited to, the evidence of the children's guardian. The court is the decision maker and must reach its decision by reference to the matters set out in the Children Act 1989 s 1 having regard to the totality of the evidence before the court.

21. FPR 2010 r 16.25 provides as follows in respect of the power of the court to terminate the appointment of a children's guardian appointed under FPR 2010 r

16.4:

16.25 Court's power to change children's guardian and prevent person acting as children's guardian

(1) The court may -

- *(a) direct that a person may not act as a children's guardian;*
- *(b) terminate the appointment of a children's guardian;*
- *(c) appoint a new children's guardian in substitution for an existing one.*

(2) An application for an order or direction under paragraph (1) must be supported by evidence.

(3) Subject to rule 16.24(6), the court may not appoint a children's guardian under this rule unless it is satisfied that the person to be appointed complies with the conditions specified in rule 16.24(5).

22. FPR 2010 PD16A para 7.17 makes clear that where an application is made for an order under FPR 2010 r 16.25 the applicant must set out the reasons for seeking it and that the application must be supported by evidence.

23. Whilst FPR 2010 r 16.25(1)(b) sets out the power of the court to terminate the appointment of the children's guardian, it articulates no criteria against which the court should consider an application for termination. When examining the almost identical provision in CPR 1998 r 21.7 dealing with the power to terminate the appointment of a litigation friend, Foskett J observed in Bradbury v Paterson [2015] COPLR 425 at [31] that the court's discretion is a full one. Within the context of determining an application to terminate the appointment of a children's guardian pursuant to FPR 2010 r 16.25(1)(b) in my judgment the following matters will be relevant to the exercise of the court's discretion.

24. Pursuant to FPR 2010 r 1.2, when exercising its power under FPR 2010 r 16.25 or interpreting FPR 2010 r 16.25 the court must seek to give effect to the overriding objective in FPR 2010 r 1.1 to deal with the case justly having regard to the welfare issues involved. Pursuant to FPR 2010 r 1.1(2) dealing with the case justly includes, so far as is practicable:

i) Ensuring that the case is dealt with expeditiously and fairly;

ii) Dealing with the case in ways which are proportionate to the nature, importance and complexity of the issues;

iii) Ensuring that the parties are on an equal footing;

iv) Saving expense; and

v) Allotting to the case an appropriate share of the court's resources while taking into account the need to allot resources to other cases.

25. There are few authorities concerning the termination of the appointment of the children's guardian. In Oxfordshire County Council v P [1995] 1 WLR 543, [1995] 1 FLR 552 Ward J (as he then was) allowed the application to terminate the appointment of the children's guardian in circumstances where the mother had disclosed to the guardian that she had caused injuries to the child and the guardian was thereafter interviewed by the Police to obtain a witness statement from her to prove criminal charges arising out of the injuries, during which interview she disclosed the mother's admissions without the leave of the court. Ward J concluded in respect of the guardian that "To encourage frankness on the part of the parents, she must be replaced even though her work in all other respects has been wholly admirable and my criticism of her is technical not substantial."

26. *In Re J (Adoption: Appointment of Guardian ad Litem) [1999] 2 FLR 86 the Court of Appeal refused an application to terminate a guardian's appointment (made within the context of an application for permission to appeal an order appointing a guardian in adoption proceedings) notwithstanding that at a meeting following the cessation of her appointment in the care proceedings, but prior to her appointment in the adoption proceedings the guardian had expressed agreement to the proposal that the child be placed for adoption. In Re J Ward LJ held that it is untenable to assert that there is bias or the appearance of bias based simply on adverse views expressed in the course of long proceedings.*

27. *Further, in Re J Ward LJ agreed with the observation of the judge at first instance that, frequently, a children's guardian holding a certain view can be persuaded under cross-examination to change their minds, that the "flexibility, rigidity, competence, balance, wisdom or other aspects of her conduct of the case are matters which the court will be invited to take into account when deciding whether to accept her evidence or recommendations" and that "Only in very rare circumstances can such factors disqualify a Guardian from acting at all". Within this context I also note the observation of*

Sir Nicholas Wall in A County Council v K, C and T [2011] 2 FLR 817 at [117] that:

> *"The reasoning of the Cafcass guardian, whether given orally or in writing is always open to challenge in cross-examination, which can always go to method. Added to which, of course, where the report is in writing, good practice requires the investigative and reasoning processes to be set out. Once again, the decision is for the court, which is heavily dependent upon the quality of the advice it receives."*

28. *Finally, in respect of Re J, at 88 Ward LJ agreed with the observations of the judge at first instance that the guardian's function is not a judicial function. In short, and once again, the court and not the children's guardian is the final arbiter of what is in the child's best interests. Within the context of this latter point, it is important, once again, to note the observations of Macur LJ in MW v Hertfordshire County Council [2014] EWCA Civ 405 at [32] that the children's guardian is a witness subject to the same judicial scrutiny as any other witness and starts with no special advantage in proceedings as compared with other witnesses.*

29. *Finally, in relation to the authorities, in Re A (Conjoined Twins: Medical Treatment)(No 2) [2001] 1 FLR 267 Ward LJ held that the court can terminate the appointment of a Children's Guardian where he or she has acted manifestly contrary to the best interests of the child, observing as follows:*

> *"It was not necessary for the President, in order to dispose of the application, to attempt any comprehensive statement of the circumstances in which it might be expedient to remove a guardian ad litem, and the President wisely did not embark on that course. Neither r 4.10(9) of the Family Proceedings Rules 1991 nor the corresponding provision of*

the Civil Procedure Rules 1998 (r 21.7(1)) specifies any limit on the court's power to terminate the appointment of a guardian ad litem or litigation friend. The President focused on the particular situation in which the court is asked to replace a guardian ad litem because the guardian has in the conduct of litigation taken a course of action (in which we include an omission), or is about to take a course of action, which is manifestly contrary to the best interests of the child whose interests it is the guardian's duty to safeguard. If the guardian (or litigation friend) does act manifestly contrary to the child's best interests, the court will remove him even though neither his good faith nor his diligence is in issue."

30. *Overall, it would appear that whilst the court's discretion to terminate the appointment of a children's guardian under FPR 2010 r 16.25(1)(b) is a full one, it is nonetheless a discretion that should be exercised sparingly, taking into account the imperative of the overriding objective in FPR 2010 r 1.1 to deal with the case justly having regard to the welfare issues involved. Within this context, where the grounds relied on in support of an application to terminate the appointment of the children's guardian concern the methodology adopted by the guardian, the court may terminate the appointment where the guardian acts manifestly contrary to the child's best interests or, but only in very rare circumstances, where the guardian has engaged in conduct that the court would ordinarily be invited simply to take into account when deciding whether to accept or reject the guardian's evidence or recommendations'.*

The above is important when considering the role of children to proceedings, both public and private. The court has the ultimate ability to terminate the appointment of the guardian. The law is comprehensive in that regard, but the guidance can be found in the above case law.

Role of the Guardian in Fact-Finding Hearings

Given the role of guardians to proceedings, the question about the role they advance or embark upon during fact-finding hearings has also been a question for the courts, specifically in the public law context. By way of brief introduction, public law cases can involve very serious allegations of harm, both physical and psychological. There are often, in the extreme cases fact-finding hearings where threshold is in dispute, for example in non-accidental injury cases. As the parents / intervenors are participating in the proceedings facing allegations, it is the local authority who have the burden upon them, to prove on the balance of probabilities the findings they seek to rely upon for the purposes of threshold. However, because of the fact that children are joined and there is a guardian appointed, the question arises as to what role the guardian should take in such proceedings.

Firstly, the matter was considered by Mr Justice Hayden in Cumbria CC v KW[12], where his lordship stated at paragraph 58:

> *'I record that the Guardian thought it appropriate not to advance any submissions on the findings sought by the Local Authority. This is a widespread practice which I would, for my part, strongly deprecate, in most cases. The importance of strong, intellectually rigorous representation on behalf of the child's lawyer and his Guardian, has been emphasised regularly see GW and PW v Oldham MBC [2005] EWCA CIV1247; Re U (A Child) [2005] 2 FLR 444; Islington LBC v Al-Alas and Rway [2012] 2 FLR 1239. These principles apply just as vigorously, in my judgement, to the fact-finding process. A position of neutrality motivated solely by desire to be independent and objective in the eyes of the parents loses sight of the primary*

12 [2016] EWHC 26 (Fam)

> *professional obligation to the child. I am aware that others take a different view.'*

As can be seen, his lordship pointed out the 'widespread practice' which was far from encouraged from the judge. There are a number of other key authorities that deal with this particular aspect. For example, in Re U (A Child)[13] Dame Butler-Sloss as she then was said the following whilst commenting on the role of the guardian from paragraph 96 onwards:

> *'We have set out above the steps taken by the solicitor for the mother to exclude the guardian from playing any part in the further expert's meeting, even to the extent of indicating that she should not even attend the meeting. We should like to express our concern that the local authority should have remained relatively neutral on this point and that 1 entitled to attempt to dispense with the guardian or marginalise the guardian on the ground that in an earlier part of the case, the guardian's recommendation had been adverse to that party (see generally independence of court welfare and guardian in Re S [1993] 1FLR 110; [1992 2 FCR 554). Other than in exceptional circumstances of specific bias or impropriety, the independence of the guardian may not be impugned as a result of the decision of the guardian to support the proposed care plan for local authority'.*

At times, it had been the practice that the guardian would seek to be 'neutral'. Dealing with this point, in GW & PW v Oldham MBC and KPW[14], Lord Justice Wall stated:

> *"Whilst a guardian, quite properly, may wish to remain neutral in a fact finding hearing, it seems to me worth remembering that the guardian (and the solicitor instructed by the guardian) do,*

---

13 [2005] 2 FLR 444

14 (A Child) [2005] EWCA Civ 1247

> *in my judgement, have a proactive role to play in ensuring that a case is ready for hearing, and that all appropriate evidence has been assembled. Accordingly, if a guardian takes the view that a second opinion sought by parents is properly necessary to achieve justice, he or she should not hesitate to say so. As I made clear in Re CB and JB (Care Proceedings: Guidelines)[1998] 2 FLR 211, 229-230, the relationship between the guardian and her solicitor needs to be intellectually rigorous, and in my judgement it is for the guardian and the solicitor he or she has instructed carefully to examine the factual sub-stratum of the case, and to advise the judge what evidence is required to enable the judge to reach a just conclusion."* (para 48).

So in practice, what should the guardian be seeking to do? The above authorities makes the position very clear, and given the increase publication rate, the role of each advocate is under scrutiny. Mrs Justice Theis set out an important task for the role of the guardian in Islington LBC v A-A and R[15] where her ladyship stated:

> *'the role of the CG can include drawing to the court's attention to all relevant matters to assist in the fact finding exercise (see Lancashire v DE [2010] 196 at para 19]. In my judgement in cases as complex as this that remains a valuable role for the CG to have. With the benefit of hindsight it is perhaps a role that should have been given more robust encouragement in this case at a CMC". (para 238)'*

Separate Representation of Children – Public Law

There are however circumstances where a child seeks separate representation. The Family Procedure Rules identifies the duties and powers of a guardian. It does however need to be emphasised that those

15 [2012] 2 FLR 1239

duties and powers will depend on how the guardian was appointed by reference to the type of proceedings. Pursuant to FPR r.16.20, a guardian appointed under 16.3 (in specified proceedings or in proceedings to which Part 14 applies) has their power and duties identified. Pursuant to FPR r.16.27, a guardian appointed in different circumstances under 16.4 (not in specified proceedings or in proceedings to which Part 14 applies) also has their power and duties are identified.

In unspecified proceedings it is the child's solicitor alone who is tasked with evaluating the child's competence to understand the proceedings and to give instruction directly (for example see FPR 2010 r 16.6(3). In specified proceedings, such as public law care proceedings, the solicitor must take into account the views of the Guardian or direction of the court in this evaluation (see FPR 2010 r 16. 29 (3).

Firstly, practitioners must have regard to Rule 16.6 which outlines the following:

'16.6 Circumstances in which a child does not need a children's guardian or litigation friend

(1) Subject to paragraph (2), a child may conduct proceedings without a children's guardian or litigation friend where the proceedings are proceedings –

(a) under the 1989 Act;

(b) to which Part 11 (applications under Part 4A of the Family Law Act 1996 or Part 1 of Schedule 2 to the Female Genital Mutilation Act 2003) or Part 14 (applications in adoption, placement and related proceedings) of these rules apply;

(c) relating to the exercise of the court's inherent jurisdiction with respect to children; or

(d) under section 55A of the 1986 Act,

and one of the conditions set out in paragraph (3) is satisfied.

(2) Paragraph (1) does not apply where the child is the subject of and a party to proceedings –

(a) which are specified proceedings; or

(b) to which Part 14 applies.

(3) The conditions referred to in paragraph (1) are that either –

(a) the child has obtained the court's permission; or

(b) a solicitor –

(i) considers that the child is able, having regard to the child's understanding, to give instructions in relation to the proceedings; and

(ii) has accepted instructions from that child to act for that child in the proceedings and, if the proceedings have begun, the solicitor is already acting.

(4) An application for permission under paragraph (3)(a) may be made by the child without notice.

(5) Where a child –

(a) has a litigation friend or children's guardian in proceedings to which this rule applies; and

(b) wishes to conduct the remaining stages of the proceedings without the litigation friend or children's guardian,

the child may apply to the court, on notice to the litigation friend or children's guardian, for permission for that purpose and for the removal of the litigation friend or children's guardian.

(6) The court will grant an application under paragraph (3)(a) or (5) if it considers that the child has sufficient understanding to conduct the proceedings concerned or proposed without a litigation friend or children's guardian.

(7) In exercising its powers under paragraph (6) the court may require the litigation friend or children's guardian to take such part in the proceedings as the court directs.

(8) The court may revoke any permission granted under paragraph (3)(a) where it considers that the child does not have sufficient understanding to participate as a party in the proceedings concerned without a litigation friend or children's guardian.

(9) Where a solicitor is acting for a child in proceedings without a litigation friend or children's guardian by virtue of paragraph (3)(b) and either of the conditions specified in paragraph (3)(b)(i) or (ii) cease to be fulfilled, the solicitor must inform the court immediately.

(10) Where –

(a) the court revokes any permission under paragraph (8); or

(b) either of the conditions specified in paragraph (3)(b)(i) or (ii) is no longer fulfilled,

> *the court may, if it considers it necessary in order to protect the interests of the child concerned, appoint a person to be that child's litigation friend or children's guardian'*

The law was reviewed by Mr Justice Williams in CS v SBH & Ors (Appeal FPR 16.5: Sufficiency of Child's Understanding)[16]. As the name of the judgment outlines, the case considers the aspect of '*sufficiency of child's understanding*'. As the judge outlined in the judgment (at paragraph 39) in areas of dispute, as to whether the child has understanding or sufficient understanding to conduct proceedings without the guardian, it is a matter for the court. The judge within the judgment, the judge reviewed all the significant authorities and stated the following at paragraph 50 onwards:

> *50. 'I now turn then to the meaning of 'sufficient understanding to conduct the proceedings.' As I have already noted the terms 'able, having regard to the child's understanding to give instructions' and 'sufficient understanding to conduct the proceedings' are subtly different, albeit as the Court of Appeal concluded in Re S (above) in practice in most cases will involve an application of the same test and will result in the same outcome. The shorthands of 'sufficient understanding' and 'understanding' have been used interchangeably in the jurisprudence and in practice professionals often refer to whether the child is 'competent' to instruct a solicitor without a Guardian or has 'capacity' so to do. All ultimately are referring to the same substantive issue. The sufficient understanding formula also applies for applications by a child for leave to bring an application under section 8 of the children act 1989: see section 10 (8).*
>
> *51. Although the subject matter of the case was the child's ability to consent to medical treatment the decision of the House of Lords*

16 [2019] EWHC 634 (Fam)

in Gillick v West Norfolk and Wisbech AHA [1985] UKHL 7 [1986] AC 112 remains the cornerstone of our current approach to questions relating to the capacity or competence of a child or young person to take decisions for themselves. Whilst the court retains the ability to, in effect, override a child's 'decision' where it considers that decision is not in the child's best interests that is a quite separate matter to the issue of whether the child is competent. Lord Scarman observed:

[186] The underlying principle of the law was exposed by Blackstone and can be seen to have been acknowledged in the case-law. It is that parental right yields to the child's right to make his own decisions when he reaches a sufficient understanding and intelligence to be capable of making up his own mind on the matter requiring decision.

[188] … The House must, in my view, be understood as having in that case accepted that, save where statute otherwise provides, a minor's capacity to make his or her own decision depends upon the minor having sufficient understanding and intelligence to make the decision and is not to be determined by reference to any judicially fixed age limit…

[189] …I would hold that as a matter of law the parental right to determine whether or not their minor child below the age of 16 will have medical treatment terminates if and when the child achieves a sufficient understanding and intelligence to enable him or her to understand fully what is proposed. It will be a question of fact whether a child seeking advice has sufficient understanding of what is involved to give a consent valid in law. Until the child achieves the capacity to consent, the parental right to make the decision continues save only in exceptional circumstances."

The key expression which emerges from those passages but which are reflected in the judgment of Lord Fraser also are 'sufficient understanding and intelligence' to make the decision.

52. In Re S (A Minor) (Independent Representation) - [1993] 2 FLR 437 the Court of Appeal considered the House of Lords judgments in Gillick and specifically with reference to the expressions 'understanding' or 'sufficient understanding' under FPR 9.2A the 1991 rules said

(3) The tests in paras (1)(b)(i) and (6) are framed with reference to the child's understanding, not his age. In the ordinary way it is no doubt true (at least of children) that understanding increases with the passage of time. But the rule eschews any arbitrary line of demarcation based on age, and wisely so. Different children have differing levels of understanding at the same age. And understanding is not an absolute. It has to be assessed relatively to the issues in the proceedings. Where any sound judgment on these issues calls for insight and imagination which only maturity and experience can bring, the child to the court and the solicitor will be slow to conclude that the child's understanding is sufficient.

53. In Re CT (A Minor) (Wardship: Representation) [1993] 2 FLR 278, [1994] Fam 49, [1993] 3 WLR 602, CA Court of Appeal (Sir Thomas Bingham MR, Waite and Staughton LLJ) endorsed the approach of Sir Thomas Bingham MR in Re S (above) and thereafter referred to the child capability and understanding. The Court said:

'I would hope and expect that instances where a challenge is directed to a solicitor's view of his minor client's ability to instruct him will be rare, and that cases where the court felt bound to question such ability of its own motion would be rarer still. If and when such instances do arise, I would expect them to be resolved by a swift, pragmatic inquiry conducted in a manner which involved the minimum delay and the least possible distress to the child concerned.

It would be very unsatisfactory if such issues themselves became the subject of detailed medical or other professional investigation. My own experience in this field of the law suggests that judges can be trusted to use their powers under rule 9.2A(10) sensitively, recognising that in border-line cases the solicitor's view should be entitled to the benefit of the doubt; and that solicitors, for their part, can be expected to appreciate that appraisal of a minor's capability to give instructions may often represent a difficult task in which objectivity and precision are not easily achieved, and to be ready to acknowledge, and even welcome, a second opinion.'

54. In <u>Re N (Contact: Minor Seeking Leave to Defend and Removal of a Guardian)</u> [2003] 1 FLR 652 Coleridge J stated (emphasis added)

'The most helpful encapsulation of the case-law I find to be that of Booth J in the case of Re H (A Minor) (Guardian ad Litem: Requirement) [1994] Fam 11, sub nom Re H (A Minor) (Role of Official Solicitor) [1993] 2 FLR 552 reading from 13 and 554H respectively. She said this:

'The approach to be taken by a court to an application such as this was fully canvassed by the Court of Appeal in Re S (A Minor) (Independent Representation) [1993] 2 FLR 437, in which judgment was delivered on 26 February 1993. The test is clear. The court must be satisfied that H, in this instance, has sufficient understanding to participate as a party in the proceedings without a guardian ad litem. Participating as a party, in my judgment, means much more than instructing a solicitor as to his own views. The child enters the arena amongst other adult parties. He may give evidence and he may be cross-examined. He will hear other parties, including in this case his parents, give evidence and be cross-examined. He must be able to give instructions on many different matters as the case goes through its stages and to make decisions as need arises. Thus a child is exposed and not protected in these procedures. It has yet to be

determined how far the court has power, if it has any power, in such circumstances to deny a child access to the hearing. The child also will be bound to abide by the rules which govern other parties, including rules as to confidentiality.'

I find that a very succinct and useful statement of the law, relying as it does upon the very clear statement of the law set out by the Master of the Rolls in Re S (A Minor) (Independent Representation) [1993] Fam 263, [1993] 2 FLR 437, relying as he did upon a passage in an unreported case of Thorpe J called Re T (A Minor), 28 January 1993, where Thorpe J, as he then was, said in proceedings launched under r 9(2)A by a 13 year old without a guardian:

'I am bound to say that in an issue of this great complexity and with a child of only 13 years of age, I doubt whether on an application for leave I would have been persuaded that she had sufficient understanding to participate without the aid of a guardian. In a case of this sort, which was referred to the High Court with much complexity and delicacy, I would have certainly regarded the Official Solicitor as the appropriate guardian ad litem.'

I have been referred to a number of other cases. I do not think they take the matter, so far as the law is concerned, any further in relation to this particular issue. Each child and each case has to be looked at separately."

55. *In Mabon v Mabon [2005] EWCA Civ 634 Thorpe LJ made the following observation at paragraphs 28-29:*

"The guidance given by this court in Re: S cited above on the construction of rule 9.2A is now twelve years old. Much has happened in that time. Although the United Kingdom had ratified the UN Convention some fifteen months earlier, it did not have much impact initially and it is hardly surprising that it was not mentioned by this court on the 26th February 1993. Although the tandem model has many strengths and virtues, at its heart lies the conflict between

advancing the welfare of the child and upholding the child's freedom of expression and participation. Unless we in this jurisdiction are to fall out of step with similar societies as they safeguard Article 12 rights, we must, in the case of articulate teenagers, accept that the right to freedom of expression and participation outweighs the paternalistic judgment of welfare.

In testing the sufficiency of a child's understanding I would not say that welfare has no place. If direct participation would pose an obvious risk of harm to the child are arising out of the nature of the continuing proceedings and, if the child is incapable of comprehending that risk, then the judge is entitled to find that sufficient understanding has not been demonstrated. But judges have to be equally alive to the risk of emotional harm that might arise from denying the child knowledge of and participation in the continuing proceedings"

[32] In conclusion, this case provides a timely opportunity to recognise the growing acknowledgement of the autonomy and consequential rights of children, both nationally and internationally. The FPR are sufficiently robustly drawn to accommodate that shift. In individual cases, trial judges must equally acknowledge that shift when they make a proportionate judgment of the sufficiency of the child's understanding.

56. *In Re W (A Child) (Care Proceedings: Child's Representation) Practice Note [2016] EWCA Civ 1051, [2017] 1 WLR 1027) the Court of Appeal was considering an appeal in relation to FPR 16.29 (2). In that case the child who had been subject to care proceedings had been separately represented by her solicitor because her position conflicted with the Guardian and her solicitor considered she was able having regard to her understanding to give instructions on her own behalf. In later proceedings a Guardian was appointed who appointed a solicitor. The child wished to instruct her own solicitor directly. There was a dispute between the view of the solicitor*

instructed by the child and the Guardian and the solicitor appointed by the Guardian as to whether the child was competent to instruct a solicitor directly. The first instance judge concluded that she did not have the capacity to instruct her own solicitor directly. The child appealed to the Court of Appeal against that conclusion'.

The judge also summarised the conclusions of Lady Justice Black, at paragraph 58 when summarising the following principles:

58. *'Lady Justice Black reviewed recent authorities addressing the understanding required of a child before she is considered able to give instructions from paragraphs 23 to 26. She identified the sea-change in attitudes over the years towards children's participation in proceedings and the autonomy and consequential rights of children and that process continued apace. Drawing the threads of her review together she said:*

[27] The question of whether a child is able, having regard to his or her understanding, to instruct a solicitor must be approached having in mind this acknowledgement of the autonomy of children and of the fact that it can at times be in their interests to play some direct part in the litigation about them. What is sufficient understanding in any given case will depend upon all the facts. In this particular case, in my judgment, the criticisms made by Ms Giz of Her Honour Judge Williams' approach, taken together, fatally undermine the decision that she took. The careful submissions on behalf of the local authority and the guardian in support of her determination failed to persuade me otherwise.

[36] Sometimes there will be a clear answer to the question whether the child is able, having regard to his or her understanding, to give their own instructions to a solicitor. In cases of more difficulty, the court will have to take a down to earth approach to determining the issue, avoiding too sophisticated an examination of the position and recognising

that it is unlikely to be desirable (or even possible) to attempt to assemble definitive evidence about the matter at this stage of the proceedings. All will depend upon the individual circumstances of the case and it is impossible to provide a route map to the solution. However, it is worth noting particularly that, given the public funding problems, the judge will have to be sure to take whatever steps are possible to ensure that the child's point of view in relation to separate representation is sufficiently before the court. The judge will expect to be guided by the guardian and by those solicitors who have formed a view as to whether they could accept instructions from the child. Then it will be for the judge to form his or her own view on the material available at that stage in the proceedings, sometimes (but certainly not always) including expert opinion on the question of understanding (see Re H (A Minor) (Care Proceedings: Child's Wishes) *[1993] 1 FLR 440, at 450). Understanding can be affected by all sorts of things, including the age of the child, his or her intelligence, his or her emotional and/or psychological and/or psychiatric and/or physical state, language ability, influence etc. The child will obviously need to comprehend enough of what the case is about (without being expected to display too sophisticated an understanding) and must have the capacity to give his or her own coherent instructions, without being more than usually inconsistent. If the judge requires an expert report to assist in determining the question of understanding, the child should be under no illusions about the importance of keeping the appointment with the expert concerned. It is an opportunity for the child to demonstrate that he or she does have the necessary understanding and there is always a risk that a failure to attend will be taken to show a failure to understand.*

59. Lady Justice Black identified particular issues giving rise to difficulties in the evaluation of understanding as including:

i) The risk of placing too much weight in the evaluation of the child's understanding of allegations of influence or manipulation of the child by a parent,

ii) The fact that a child's views may be considered to be misguided does not necessarily mean the child does not have sufficient understanding to instruct a solicitor.

iii) The danger of the court becoming too embroiled in consideration of i) and ii) above such that it pre-judges what may be central issues in the substantive application.

iv) The need to balance the harm that might be caused by direct participation with the harm that might be caused by refusal of direct participation.

60. *I was also referred to the decision of Mr Justice Peter Jackson (as he then was) in S v S (Relocation) [2017] EWHC 2345 (Fam), [2018] 1 FLR 825. The situation in which children are taken secretly by one parent (or grandparent) to see a solicitor either in advance of or in the course of an application or following an unsuccessful outcome is a matter which can cause profound concern. As HHJ Meston QC identified and as is emphasised by Ms Hopkin and Mr Burrows a competent child who wishes to instruct a solicitor has the same right to do so as any other individual. Orders directed at the child herself or a solicitor she wishes to instruct which have the effect of inhibiting or preventing that right raise very serious issues which do not call for determination in this case. Orders directed at the parents in the form of prohibited steps orders or specific issue orders and which are designed to inhibit or prevent them from assisting or encouraging a child to obtain legal advice are a different matter. In the course of the hearings on both 13 February 2019 and 26 February 2019 it was suggested that the order made by HHJ Meston QC on 6 November 2018 prohibited the child from seeing Ms Hopkin or Mr Burrows. Neither paragraph 11 nor*

paragraph 12 of the order had that effect and as is clear from paragraph 114 of HHJ Meston QC's judgment they were not intended to do so. As I have referred to above Ms Hopkin appeared pro bono because she was concerned at the potential conflict or appearance thereof that being funded by the mother might create. Again it is not an issue that I need to determine in this judgment but I acknowledge that there is some debate about the issue of one parent (perhaps with their own agenda) funding the obtaining of legal advice by a child who they believe is aligned with their position. The significance of the S-v-S decision lies in the further recognition of the importance of the autonomy of the child'.

Taking together all the threads, the judge summarised the assessment for determination at paragraph 64 as follows:

'Thus in determining whether the child has sufficient understanding to give instructions to pursue an appeal and to conduct the appeal I need to consider a range of factors including

i) The level of intelligence of the child

ii) The emotional maturity of the child.

iii) Factors which might undermine their understanding such as issues arising from their emotional, psychological, psychiatric or emotional state.

iv) Their reasons for wishing to instruct a solicitor directly or to act without a guardian and the strength of feeling accompanying the wish to play a direct role.

v) Their understanding of the issues in the case and their desired outcome any matter which sheds light on the extent to which those are authentically their own or are mere parroting of one parent's position. Some degree of influence is a natural component of decision making but the closer to the 'parroting' end of the spectrum one gets the lower the level of understanding there is likely to be. An unwise decision does not mean the child does not understand although it will no doubt depend on the extent to which the child's view diverges from an objectively reasonable or wise decision.

vi) *Their understanding of the process of litigation including the function of their lawyer, the role of the judge, the role they might play and the law that is applied and some of the consequences of involvement in litigation. Care should be taken not to impose too high a level of understanding in this regard; many adults with capacity would not and we should not expect it from children. An ability to understand that their solicitor put their case but also has duties of honesty to the court, an ability to understand that the judge makes a decision based on an overall evaluation of the best interests of the child which balances many competing factors; the ability to understand that they might attend court, could give and evidence, could read documents; the ability to recognise the stress of exposure to the court process and the arguments between others. The presence of all of these would be powerful signs of a high level of understanding. Conversely the absence of them or evidence of a distorted understanding would be contra-indicators.*

vii) *The court's assessment of the risk of harm to the child of direct participation for the risk of harm arising from excluding the child from direct participation and the child's appreciation of the risks of harm.*

> 65. *Ideally the assessment would be swift and pragmatic without too deep a dive into the issues in the case and the competing analyses of the solicitors involved. In some cases, an expert assessment might be required in particular where the solicitors' assessments are relatively evenly balanced or the court is otherwise unable to reach a clear view. No party suggested an expert was required in this case'.*

It can be taken from William J's authority that any assessment is required to be swift and pragmatic without a deep dive into the issues with competing analysis, which can sometimes arise. An expert assessment may be required in certain situations where a solicitors' assessment is fairly evenly balanced or if the court required one as necessary because of an inability to take a view on the evidence. Since this judgment, there have been various other judgments considering the issue.

Conclusion of Chapter

Public law proceedings are unique in one sense, that children are directly involved as a guardian is appointed when a local authority intervenes and issues an application for an interim care order or interim supervision order. Having a guardian, does provide a vessel for the children to directly participate in the proceedings. This chapter does outline, there can be difficulties that can arise with an application to terminate a guardian or issues relating to separate representation arising. The case law has developed in a manner where it is essential that practitioners are fully on top of the issues, in case any issues arise in the proceedings.

CHAPTER FOUR

INTERNATIONAL PROCEEDINGS AND CHILDREN PARTICIPATION

Introduction to the Chapter

International children law applies different, but similar concepts to private and public law proceedings. Particularly where the 1980 Hague Convention applies, as this chapter will outline. However, in proceedings concerning the inherent jurisdiction, the law is domestic, i.e the best interests of the child. Therefore, the participation of children is very similar to public and private law proceedings. There are however, unique rules in existence when it comes to children representation in 1980 Hague Convention cases, which came under scrutiny in a landmark joint appeal in the summer of 2023.

1980 Hague Convention Proceedings – Role of the Children

One successful international treaty is the 1980 Hague Convention. This Convention has a number of signatories, approximately close to 100 countries. The Convention sets out clearly in Article 1 a clear aim:

> *'The objects of the present Convention are -*
>
> *a) to secure the prompt return of children wrongfully removed to or retained in any Contracting State; and*

> *b) to ensure that rights of custody and of access under the law of one Contracting State are effectively respected in the other Contracting States'*

Further, Article 2 and 11 sets out the need for proceedings under the 1980 Hague Convention to be dealt with expeditiously. Article 2 states:

> *'Contracting States shall take all appropriate measures to secure within their territories the implementation of the objects of the Convention. For this purpose they shall use the most expeditious procedures available'*

Article 11 states:

> *'The judicial or administrative authorities of Contracting States shall act expeditiously in proceedings for the return of children.*
>
> *If the judicial or administrative authority concerned has not reached a decision within six weeks from the date of commencement of the proceedings, the applicant or the Central Authority of the requested State, on its own initiative or if asked by the Central Authority of the requesting State, shall have the right to request a statement of the reasons for the delay. If a reply is received by the Central Authority of the requested State, that Authority shall transmit the reply to the Central Authority of the requesting State, or to the applicant, as the case may be'.*

It is therefore apparent from its language; the Convention is a strict treaty with focused aims. It outlined the impact upon child abduction and how states who are signatories to the Convention must act expeditiously in determining a 1980 Hague Convention.

In England, 1980 Hague Convention cases are heard in the High Court also. For example, if a child is abducted from a signatory to the Convention to this country, the proceedings will commence in the High Court and remain there until the conclusion of the proceedings. High

Court judges are therefore particularly experienced at dealing with child abduction matters. The provisions are often regarded as being interpreted narrowly because the aim is to return children to the country of their habitual residence. The Convention considers in detail what is regarded as wrongful removal or wrongful retention and what the exceptions to a summary return are. Perhaps the matter can be explained nicely by Mostyn J in B v B[17] where his lordship stated:

> '*2 The Hague Convention of 1980 is arguably the most successful ever international treaty and it has over 90 subscribers to it, over half the countries in the world. The underlying and central foundation of the Convention is that, where a child has been unilaterally removed from the land of her habitual residence in breach of someone's rights of custody, then she should be swiftly returned to that country for the courts of that country to decide on her long*-term future.
>
> *3 There are very few exceptions to this and the exceptions that do exist have to be interpreted very narrowly in order that the central premise of the Convention is not fatally undermined. It is important to understand what the Convention does not do. The Convention does not order a child who has been removed in the circumstances I have described to live with anybody. The Convention does not provide that the parent who is left behind should, on the return of the child, have contact or access in any particular way. The Convention does not provide that, when an order for return to the child's homeland is made, the child should stay there indefinitely. All the Convention provides is that the child should be returned for the specific purpose and limited period to enable the court of her homeland to decide on her long-term future. That is all it decides.*

---

17 [2014] EWHC 1804

> *4 ... Equally, if the exception that is relied on is that there is a grave risk that his or her return would expose the child to physical or psychological harm or otherwise place her in an intolerable situation, that again has to be seen through the lens of the objective of the Convention. We are not talking here about long- term risks. We are not talking here about long-term harm. We are talking about risks and harm that would eventuate only in the period that it takes for the court of the child's homeland to determine her long-term future and to impose the necessary safeguards, if necessary, in the interim.'*

Further in Re D (A Child) (Abduction: Rights of Custody)[18], Baroness Hale of Richmond observed:

> *'The whole object of the Convention is to secure the swift return of children wrongfully removed from their home country, not only so that they can return to the place which is properly their 'home', but also so that any dispute about where they should live in the future can be decided in the courts of their home country, according to the laws of their home country and in accordance with the evidence which will mostly be there rather than in the country to which they have been removed'*

There are certain defences where children will play a direct role in the proceedings, particular child objections and settlement.

Child Objections

The defence is defined in the 1980 Hague Convention as follows, at Article 13:

18 [2006] UKLH 51, para 48

'The judicial or administrative authority may also refuse to order the return of the child if it finds that the child objects to being returned and has attained an age and degree of maturity at which it is appropriate to take account of its views'.

The law governing the Court's approach to a child's objections is now well settled and remains as set out by Black LJ (as she then was) in Re M (Republic of Ireland: Child's Objections)[19] at paragraphs 34 onwards.

Particular attention is drawn to paragraphs 69-71 of Black LJ's judgement (agreed by the other two members of the Court of Appeal). It is submitted that a three-stage process involving: -

a. "fairly low threshold" to establishing a "gateway stage". This is a factual and "straightforward" analysis of the entirety of the evidence before the court to be conducted "robustly" in "simple terms";

b. Once established the court then considers the child's age and degree of maturity in relation to whether to take account of their views; and

c. If so, the discretion is engaged and stands to be considered.

Black LJ took the opportunity in Re-F (Child's Objections)[20] at paragraph 33 to confirm that:

- the current approach was to discourage an "*over prescriptive or over intellectualised approach" adopting a "straightforward" analysis of a simple question "does the child object to being returned to his or her country of habitual residence?*". Paragraph 35 confirmed that

---

[19] [2015] 2 FLR 1074

[20] [2015] EWCA Civ 1022

whether a child objects is a question of fact to be analysed on the evidence.

Lord Justices Richards and Moore-Bick expressly agreed her judgement, see paragraph 60 & 61.

In relation to the application of the test it is asserted that the following propositions can be garnered:

a. Whether the child objects to being returned is a matter of fact. So, too, is the child's age and degree of maturity.

b. There is no fixed age below at which a child's objections will not be taken into account.

c. The child's views have to amount to objections before they can give rise to an Article 13 exception. Anything less than an objection will not do.

d. The child has to object to returning to the country of habitual residence, rather than the particular circumstances in that country though the two may be difficult to separate.

e. There may be cases in which objections to returning to the country are so inevitably and inextricably linked with an objection to living with the other parent that the two factors cannot be separated. This is relevant to the discretion rather than the gateway stage.

f. A straightforward and robust process is required. The judge must simply ask himself 'Does the child object to being returned to his or her country of habitual residence'?

g. The context in which a child's views are expressed – whether or not they were formed in a 'bubble of respite' – can be relevant in evaluating those views though there is no separate test when determining whether or not the child's objections exception is established.

h. If the gateway is established the range of considerations that enters into the exercise of the discretion whether to order a summary return is wide.

If a child is found to object to a return a return, then the gateway stage relating to discretion is opened. The classic expression of the Court's discretion in a child objections defence remains as described by Baroness Hale in Re M (Zimbabwe) at paragraph 46, namely:

> *"In child's objections cases, the range of considerations may be even wider than those in the other exceptions. The exception itself is brought into play when only two conditions are met: first, that the child herself objects to being returned and second, that she has attained an age and degree of maturity at which it is appropriate to take account of her views. These days, and especially in the light of article 12 of the United Nations Convention on the Rights of the Child, courts increasingly consider it appropriate to take account of a child's views. Taking account does not mean that those views are always determinative or even presumptively so.* ***Once the discretion comes into play, the court may have to consider the nature and strength of the child's objections, the extent to which they are "authentically her own" or the product of the influence of the abducting parent, the extent to which they coincide or are at odds with other considerations which are relevant to her welfare, as well as the general Convention considerations referred to earlier. The older the child, the greater the weight that her objections are likely to carry.*** *But that is far from saying that the child's objections should only prevail in the most exceptional circumstances."* **(writer's emphasis)**

In ES v LS[21] Mostyn J held as follows with regards to the exercise of discretion where a "Gillick" competent child objected to a summary return. At paragraph 79:

> "*The discretion in this sphere is not one which will almost invariably be driven by the primary threshold condition, as is the case where risk of harm, or settlement is proved. It is a genuine discretion, but one in which the objections will weigh very heavily where they are expressed by children of this age. No one is suggesting that these children should be separated and so they have to be treated as a unit when weighing their objections. Within that unit the older child is 14½ years old. She is unquestionably Gillick competent and so her wishes will normally be decisive in any non-medical dispute that she may have with her parents: see NHS Trust v X (In the matter of X (A Child) (No 2))* [2021] EWHC 65 (Fam) *at para 30 per Sir James Munby. I accept that these proceedings are governed by a self-contained set of special rules, and that those rules do not give decisive weight to objections from a Gillick competent child.* ***However, it seems to me that when weighing a child's objections under the Convention due regard should be had to the universal policy that underpins the Gillick principle namely that a child who has achieved a sufficient degree of maturity should have her decisions about her life respected, provided that they are not foolish or irrational.*** *Whatever the nature of the proceedings it seems to me that Lord Denning's famous dictum in Hewer v Bryant [1970] 1 QB 357 at 369 should be kept in mind:*

21 [2021] EWHC 2758 (Fam)

Child Objections in Practice

As the authorities outline, whether a child objections defence exist requires it to be considered by both the court and assessed by Cafcass. At the first hearing in 1980 Hague Convention cases, particularly those on notice it is the duty of the lawyers to timetable a Cafcass report. The authorities make this clear. In Re F (Abduction: Child's Wishes it was stated:

> *'But a clear distinction has to be drawn between obligations that flow from a pleading of the child's objections and the court's obligation, quite apart from anything that may be pleaded, in all cases to hear the child, unless that necessity is excused by reference to the child's age and understanding.'*

A duty exists to lawyers and the court to ensure this issue is dealt with. Normally in practice, any child beyond the age of 7 will be assessed for a Cafcass child objections report. This report can take between 4 – 7 weeks. The Cafcass officer will be called to give oral evidence if the objections are challenged. In any event, if objections are found to be met there is a discretion in existence. There are various cases published where a discretion has been found to be met, but for other discretion reasons related to the facts of the case and policy, a return has been ordered. This happened fairly recently for example in: Re Z (A Child) (1980 Hague Convention)[22].

The child's objections defence has however raised a number of key principles about the rights and participation of children in family proceedings. For example in In Re D (A Child)[23] at paragraph 53, Baroness Hale observed:

22 [2023] EWCH 2696 (Fam).

23 [2007] 1 AC 619

> *"But there is now a growing understanding of the importance of listening to the children involved in children's cases.* ***It is the child, more than anyone else, who will have to live with what the court decides. Those who do listen to children understand that they often have a point of view which is quite distinct from that of the person looking after them.*** *They are quite capable of being moral actors in their own right. Just as the adults may have to do what the court decides whether they like it or not, so may the child. But that is no more a reason for failing to hear what the child has to say than it is for refusing to hear the parent' views."*

In Re LC (Reunite: International Child Abduction Centre Intervening)[24] , Lord Wilson made clear the same regulation applies to the 2010 FPR: *[46] Rule 16.2, set out above, governs the grant to a child of party status in family proceedings generally. There is no special provision in Pt 16 of the Rules which governs the grant to a child of party status in proceedings under the Convention. Rule 16.4(1)(c) proceeds to provide that, without prejudice to other rules, and in particular to r 16.6, a court which has granted party status to a child pursuant to r 16.2 must appoint a children's guardian for her.* The duties of the guardian, once appointed, are set out in *Practice Direction 16A— Representation of Children* ("PD16A"), paragraphs 7.6 and 7.7.

In Re C (Abduction: Separate Representation of Children)[25] Mr Justice Ryder as he was, observed the following in relation to the engagement of children within proceedings:

> *"It is persuasively argued before me that it would be emotionally harmful for the court not to empower these children not only to put their views before the court but also to have them properly, independently and specifically, advocated. However expert any*

24 [2014] UKSC 1

25 [2008] 2 FLR 6

> *CAFCASS officer may be in obtaining a child's views, much will depend on the way that officer elicits those views i.e. what questions he asks and how he interprets the answers. That officer is not able to advocate a child's views within the proceedings and in particular to respond to evidence and submissions as they unfold, giving the child's position where appropriate. The process of reporting does not allow a child to engage in the proceedings..."*

Mostyn J in IAS v CPW[26] at paragraph 44_commented:

> *'was surprised by this. Of course, had Ms Magson recommended that B should be separately represented, that would inevitably have caused an adjournment of the final hearing listed only 11 days later. It would have been impossible to have appointed a Guardian, solicitors and counsel for B and for them to have read into the case in that short period. Even so, it is surprising, given the importance of the decision for B, a Gillick-competent child, that it was thought that the case could be conducted without his case being professionally and forensically put by representatives on his behalf. FPR PD 16A para 7.2(e) cites the situation where an older child is opposing a proposed course of action as one circumstance justifying the making of an award of party status to the child. It was this particular paragraph that Lord Wilson referred to in Re LC (Children)* [2014] UKSC 1, [2014] 1 AC 1038 *at [54] when cautioning against the routine grant of party status to older children objecting to an outward return order under the Hague Convention. However, it seems to me that where an older child is settled in another place, and strongly and consistently objects to a proposed inward return order under the inherent powers of the High Court, then that situation is*

26 [2020] 4 WLR 127

> *markedly different. In my judgment, in an ideal world, B should have been awarded party status'*

In the child objections report, the Cafcass officer normally recommends if the child wishes to meet the trial judge or write a letter to the court which will form part of the Cafcass report. The Cafcass officer will be the first individual to specifically advise on separate representation. However, in cases of certain complexity such as where there is an asylum claim, there is specific guidance involving children representation and the guidance outlines that children should be joined immediately. This guidance appears at Annex 2 of the President's Guidance, titled 'Practice Guidance: Case Management and Mediation of International Child Abduction Proceedings' released in March 2023.

Settlement – 1980 Hague Convention

The next area where a child is directly involved in 1980 Hague Convention proceedings is the defence of settlement.

The wording in Article 12 states as follows:

> *'Where a child has been wrongfully removed or retained in terms of Article 3 and, at the date of the commencement of the proceedings before the judicial or administrative authority of the Contracting State where the child is, a period of less than one year has elapsed from the date of the wrongful removal or retention, the authority concerned shall order the return of the child forthwith.*
>
> *The judicial or administrative authority, even where the proceedings have been commenced after the expiration of the period of one year referred to in the preceding paragraph, shall also order the return of the child, unless it is demonstrated that the child is now settled in its new environment.*

> *Where the judicial or administrative authority in the requested State has reason to believe that the child has been taken to another State, it may stay the proceedings or dismiss the application for the return of the child'.*

In terms of when the date stops running in terms of when the issue of settlement can be considered, Re N (Minors) (Abduction)[27] infers it is the date in which the application was issued and also, as outlined by Wilson LJ at para 54 of Re O (Abduction: Settlement)[28]. In terms of the timeline for the court in respect of settlement, Mostyn J in ES v LS considered the authorities (domestic and international in detail at paragraph 52 – 69 and concluded: '*Having looked at the matter carefully, I am convinced that 'now' means 'as at the date of trial'.*

Sir Mark Potter in Re C (Child Abduction: Settlement)[29] outlines that the evidence must show that '*the present situation imports stability when looking into the future*'.

Further guidance and in particular in relation to the test of what is settlement for the purposes of Article 12 is to be found in AH v CD, London Borough of Haringey, B (Through his Guardian, Mr William Walker), W (Through the Official Solicitor)[30] (Fam) at paragraphs 41-42

> *'41. The courts have considered the principles of settlement in a number of cases, the principal amongst which are (a) Re N (Minors) (Abduction) [1991] 1 FLR 413, (b) Cannon v Cannon [2005] 1 FLR 169; (c) C v C [2006] 2 FLR 797; (d) Re M (Zimbabwe) [2008] 1 FLR 251. A recent example of the application of the principles is Re T (A Child - Hague*

---

27 [1991] 1 FCR 765

28 [2011] 2 FLR 1307

29 [2007] 1 FCR 649

30 [2018] EWHC 1643

Convention proceedings) [2016] EWHC 3554 (Fam). The principles which can be derived from those cases are these:

(i) The proceedings must be commenced within one year of the abduction. The making of a complaint to police or an application to a Central Authority does not suffice.

(ii) The focus must be on the child. Settlement must be considered from the child's perspective, not the adult's. The date for the assessment is that date of the commencement of proceedings not the date of the hearing. This is aimed at preventing settlement being achieved by delay in the process.

(iii) Settlement involves both physical and emotional or psychological components. Physically, it involves being established or integrated into an environment compromising a home and school, a social and family network, activities, opportunities. Emotional or psychological settlement connotes security and stability within that environment. It is more than mere adjustment to present surroundings.

(iv) Concealment and delay may be relevant to establishing settlement. Concealment is likely to undermine settlement. Living openly is likely to permit greater settlement. The absence of a relationship with a left behind parent will be an important consideration in determining whether a child is settled.

(v) A broad and purposive construction will properly reflect the facts of each case – it does not require a 2-stage approach but must, to use a probably over-used expression involve a holistic assessment of whether the child is settled in its new environment. It has to be kept in mind that the settlement exception is intended to

> *reflect welfare. The article 12 settlement exception of all the exceptions is most welfare focused. The underlying purpose of the exception is to enable the court in furtherance of the welfare of the child to decline a summary return because imposing a summary return (i.e. without a more detailed consideration of welfare) might compound the harm caused by the original abduction by uprooting a child summarily from his by now familiar environment.*

> *42. As I have said earlier, there is clearly a degree of overlap between the concepts of settlement and habitual residence. Settlement does not require a complete settlement, any more than habitual residence requires full integration. Settlement is plainly an evaluation which is, to some degree, subjective. There will be a spectrum ranging from the obviously and completely settled to the very unsettled. In between there are many possibilities'.*

In practice, a settlement report will also provide the child's wishes and feelings and also raise the issue of meeting the trial judge and / or separate representation.

Recent Guidance – Participation of Children in 1980 Hague Convention Proceedings

Two cases were heard jointly. Firstly, Re D (A Child) (Abduction: Child's Objections: Representation of Child Party)[31] ['Re D'] and the second case, C v M (A Child) (Abduction: Representation of Child Party)[32] ['C v M']. The Association of Lawyers for Children and Reunite International Child Abduction Centre intervened in the case.

---

[31] [2023] EWCA CIV 1047

[32] [2023] EWCA CIV 1449

Dealing with Re D first, the child was represented by a solicitor who was also appointed by the court as his guardian in the proceedings. It is recorded in the judgment that at the start of the proceedings that the mother's solicitors gave notice of the hearing to the solicitor for D [paragraph 17]. An application was made the day before for D to be joined as a party [paragraph 18].

The case concerned an appeal from the return order made on 26 May 2023 by Mr Dexter Dias KC, sitting as a Deputy High Court Judge. The judge found that D objected to being returned to Singapore but exercised his discretion by making a return order. The issue of the appeal was set out in paragraph 3:

> *'the broad issue which potentially appeared to be raised by this appeal was the role of a solicitor who is also acting as a child's guardian (a role which I give the shorthand, "solicitor-guardian") in 1980 Convention proceedings. In particular, are there constraints on the scope of the evidence they can give, for example as to their assessment of the strength or source of a child's views, either legally or, if not legally, as a matter of practice?'*

The grounds of appeal were:

> '(1) *The judge erred in his approach to the role of a solicitor who is also acting as guardian in proceedings under the 1980 Convention and, as a result, wrongly attached no or negligible weight to the opinions expressed by Mr Netto as to, in particular, the extent to which D's views were influenced by his father;*
>
> (2) *The judge erred in attaching little weight to the views of a Gillick-competent child on the basis that he had been exposed to the father's undue influence;*
>
> (3) *The judge was wrong in the approach he took to D's welfare when exercising his discretion'*

Issue 1 – Admissibility of Evidence from A Solicitor

In terms of the admissibility of evidence from the solicitor, the Court of Appeal commented at 76 – 78:

> *'It was clearly unfortunate that the issue of the admissibility of parts of Mr Netto's evidence was introduced by the judge during the final hearing. In my view, this affected the fairness of the proceedings and the proper determination of the application.*
>
> *No objection had been taken to the nature of Mr Netto's evidence prior to the hearing. Accordingly, this caught the parties by surprise and meant that they were not in a position properly to address it.*
>
> *78. More substantively, I do not consider it possible to conclude, as submitted by Mr Gration [KC], that the judge properly considered Mr Netto's evidence when making his decision. I acknowledge that the judge said that his "task" was to assess the weight he could give to Mr Netto's evidence. However, as referred to above, his conclusion that the weight it could be given was "negligible" was significantly based on his conclusions as to "the legal status and appropriateness of this evidence", as the judge phrased the issue'*

Issue 2 – Weight of a Gillick Competent Child Evidence

The judgment provided useful guidance on the issue of the weight to be given to a Gillick competent child. In particular, paragraph 83 of the judgment sets out:

> *'83. As to the second ground of appeal, a judge is entitled to give little weight to a Gillick-competent child's views if the judge concludes, as the judge did, that those "views have been and continue to be influenced by the inescapable pressure made by*

> *his F and the threat of separation". But for the matters referred to above, the judge would have been entitled to attach little weight to D's views.*
>
> *84. I would just add the following. First, "authentic" is typically used when a child's views are not considered to be the product of or reflecting, in particular, the influence of the taking parent. Secondly, a child's, even a Gillick-competent child's, views are but one element to be taken into account when the court is exercising its discretion. I would reject the submission made in the child's written submissions, based on what Mostyn J said, in a different context, in AS v CPW when he expanded on, or disagreed with, what Lady Black had said in Birmingham City Council v D (Equality and Human Rights Commission and others intervening) [2019] 1 WLR 5403, at [90], by saying, at [22]:*
>
> *"... it is not merely a question of giving "due regard" to the wishes of a Gillick-competent child on a particular issue. In my judgment, if the decision of the House of Lords in Gillick is not to be hollowed out, the wishes of a Gillick-competent child on a particular issue, where they are not objectively foolish or unreasonable, should normally be given effect"."*

Certainly in proceedings under the 1980 Convention, I would endorse what Lady Black said, albeit again in a very different context, namely that what is required is that "due regard" must be given to the wishes of a child.

> *85. Both of the above points are reflected in what Lady Hale said in In re M and another (Children) (Abduction: Rights of Custody) [2008] 1 AC 1288, at [46]:*
>
> *"In child's objections cases, the range of considerations may be even wider than those in the other exceptions. The exception itself is brought into play when only two conditions*

are met: first, that the child herself objects to being returned and second, that she has attained an age and degree of maturity at which it is appropriate to take account of her views. These days, and especially in the light of article 12 of the United Nations Convention on the Rights of the Child, courts increasingly consider it appropriate to take account of a child's views. Taking account does not mean that those views are always determinative or even presumptively so. Once the discretion comes into play, the court may have to consider the nature and strength of the child's objections, the extent to which they are "authentically her own" or the product of the influence of the abducting parent, the extent to which they coincide or are at odds with other considerations which are relevant to her welfare, as well as the general Convention considerations referred to earlier. The older the child, the greater the weight that her objections are likely to carry. But that is far from saying that the child's objections should only prevail in the most exceptional circumstances."

<u>The Second Part of the Appeal – C v M</u>

The facts in this appeal were similar, hence why it was heard together with Re D. The judgement being appealed was one where the discretion was not exercised, and a return was not ordered where a child had objected. The Grounds of Appeal were as follows:

'*(1) There was a material procedural irregularity when the Judge refused the proposed appellant's application to adjourn the re-hearing of his application so that the court could hear from Cafcass and so that Cafcass could comment on a number of issues relevant to the exercise of the court's discretion;*

(2) The Judge was wrong to exercise her discretion based on her welfare concerns for the child without further and updating

evidence from Cafcass based on an alleged change of circumstances for the child. She was wrong to substitute the expert, objective, child-focused opinion that would have been provided by Cafcass with the opinion evidence of the child's solicitor Janet Broadley, and written hearsay evidence from the child's head teacher;

(3) In exercising her discretion to refuse to order the return of either child to Mauritius, the Judge attributed disproportionate weight to the child's stated objection to a return, an objection that was no different in substance at the re-hearing to the objection the child had expressed in January. The Judge failed to attribute any or any appropriate weight to a number of other material considerations;

(4) The Judge was wrong not to insist that the mother confirm to the court whether, if the court ordered Y's return to Mauritius, the mother would return with one or both children; and wrong to assume the mother would not return in such circumstances;

(5) It was improper, in the exercise of her discretion, for the Judge to take into account the proposed appellant's alleged level of insight into alleged domestic abuse.'

As can be seen from the grounds of appeal raised in the appear, the manner in which evidence from a child, through a solicitor was to be treated, in the context of a 1980 Hague Convention defence was under scrutiny, This provided the Court of Appeal with the opportunity to consider various common themes and guidance, which they did under the heading of various issues.

Issue 1 – Children Representation

The Court of Appeal considered the law permitting children to be represented by a solicitor in 1980 Hague Convention proceedings. As outlined in Re D at paragraph 57, paragraph 3.6 of the Practice Guidance on Case Management and Mediation of International Child Abduction Proceedings, issued by Sir Andrew McFarlane P on 1 March 2023, "*In only a very few cases will party status* [for a child] *be necessary*". The child's voice is heard sufficiently through a report from a Cafcass Officer. This reflected Lady Hale's earlier comments in *In re D (A Child) (Abduction: Rights of Custody)* , at [60], when she said that "*Only in a few cases will full scale legal representation be necessary*".

The Court considered the Family Procedure Rules and in particular, Part 16 of the FPR 2020 outlines "*when the court will make a child a party in family proceedings". Proceedings under the 1980 Convention are "family proceedings*". On this point, in Re D, it was stated at paragraph 16:

> '*Rules 16.2 and 16.4 apply to proceedings under the 1980 Convention, because they are neither "specified proceedings" nor proceedings to which Part 14 applies. Rule 16.2(1) provides:*
>
> *"(1) The court may make a child a party to proceedings if it considers it is in the best interests of the child to do so."*
>
> *Rule 16.4(1) provides:*
>
> *"(1)*
>
> *... the court must appoint a children's guardian for a child who is the subject of the proceedings ... if–*
>
> ...
>
> *(c) the court has made the child a party in accordance with rule 16.2".*

> *61. Rule 16.5 deals with the "Requirement for a litigation friend" and provides that, except in proceedings under s. 55A of the Family Law Act 1986:*
>
> *"… where a child is –*
>
> *(a) a party to proceedings; but*
>
> *(b) not the subject of those proceedings,*
>
> *the child must have a litigation friend to conduct proceedings on the child's behalf."*
>
> *This provides that, where, as in the present case, the child is the subject of the proceedings, they do not have to have a litigation friend.*
>
> *62. Rule 16.6(1) provides that "a child may conduct proceedings without a children's guardian" when the court so permits or when a solicitor, instructed by the child, considers that the "the child is able, having regard to the child's understanding, to give instructions in relation to the proceedings". This provision, however, does not apply to proceedings under the 1980 Convention although it does apply to most other private law proceedings including proceedings under the inherent jurisdiction'*

<u>Issue 2 – Joinder – the Lacuna</u>

Reference in the judgments was made to WF v FJ (Abduction: Child's Objections)[33]. In this context, what was explored is what is referred to a 'lacuna' in the rules.

---

[33] [2011] 1 FLR 1153

In Re D, analysis was provided in respect of the lacuna noticed in the rules. Considering the case law, it was assessed at paragraph 64 of the judgment:

> *'Baker J considered this to be an anomalous lacuna because the effect was that a child could instruct a solicitor directly in summary return proceedings under the inherent jurisdiction but not summary return proceedings under the 1980 Convention. He took "the pragmatic approach" of appointing the solicitor acting for the child as her litigation friend while expressing the hope that this situation would be considered by the Family Procedure Rules Committee "in the near future". I would also note that, at [25], he said:*
>
> > *"Without wishing to lay down any rigid rules, it seems to me clearly preferable, where the time and resources permit, for the child to be seen by the Cafcass High Court Team before any decision is taken as to party status."*
>
> *65. It does not appear that the issue was considered by the Rules Committee because, although the structure of the FPR 2010 in respect of the representation of children is not the same as that under the previous rules, when r.16.4 applies, as it does in the present case, the position remains that the child must have a guardian. This is because, as referred to above, r.16.6 does not apply to proceedings under the 1980 Convention.*
>
> *66. This anomaly was referred to by Lord Wilson in Re LC when he said, at [46], that he could not "discern why, if and to the extent that it is appropriate in Convention proceedings for children to be made parties, the facility for some of them to act without a guardian has been blocked"'.*

Turning next on the history of the case, was the matter of *Ciccone v Ciccone.* In this case, MacDonald J at paragraph 70 – 71 outlined the following:

"70 An issue arose during the course of the hearing as to whether, in circumstances where a child is joined as a party to proceedings and represented by a solicitor who is also appointed his or her Guardian, it is necessary to have a report from Cafcass on the question of whether the child's objections are authentic, as opposed to the product of influence by the parent who has allegedly abducted the child, and the extent to which the objections coincide with, or at odds with the child's welfare. As I said during the course of giving my brief reasons on the evening on 23 December 2015, I would have liked to have had the opportunity to explore this issue in more depth during submissions. This was not possible due to the constraints of time.

71 Whilst the "gateway stage" of the child's objections defence is confined to a straightforward and fairly robust examination of whether the simple terms of the Convention are satisfied in that the child objects to being returned and has attained an age and degree of maturity at which it is appropriate to take account of his or her views, at the discretion stage the court must consider not only the nature and strength of the objections but a much wider range of considerations including whether they are authentic as opposed to the product of influence by the parent who has allegedly abducted the child and the extent to which the objections coincide with, or are at odds with the child's welfare (see In re M (Children)(Abduction: Rights of Custody) [2008] AC 1288; and In re M (Children) (Abduction: Child's objections) [2015] EWCA Civ 26); [2016] Fam 1.

72 Within this context, it does seem to me on the face of it (and without having heard detailed submissions on the point) that a solicitor who is representing an articulate and mature child joined to the proceedings, and who is bound to take and act on instructions from that child in advancing his or her case, might be placed in a difficult position if required by the court also to provide an evaluation of such issues as whether the objection

> *their client instructs them to advance is authentic as opposed to the product of influence by the abducting parent or as to the extent to which the objections coincide with, or are at odds with their client's welfare. This is particularly so where, as in this case, the child instructs his or her solicitor that his decision is free from influence and consistent with his welfare.*
>
> *73 In these circumstances, and whilst in no way seeking to lay down any general principle or rule, it seems to me that, notwithstanding that Rocco is represented by a solicitor who is also appointed as his Children's Guardian, the assessment of whether Rocco's objections are authentic as opposed to the product of influence by his father and the extent to which Rocco's objections coincide with, or are at odds with his welfare remains properly the task of a Cafcass officer.'*

Issue 3 – Opinion Evidence

The next issue was how opinion evidence should be treated when issues like this arise, where a child has instructed a solicitor directly. The Court provided a meaningful overview of the Civil Procedure Rules.

In particular,

Section 3 of the Civil Evidence Act 1972 provides as follows:

> *"3 Admissibility of expert opinion and certain expressions of non-expert opinion*
>
> (1) *Subject to any rules of court made in pursuance of. . . this Act, where a person is called as a witness in any civil proceedings, his opinion on any relevant matter on which he is qualified to give expert evidence shall be admissible in evidence.*

(2) *It is hereby declared that where a person is called as a witness in any civil proceedings, a statement of opinion by him on any relevant matter on which he is not qualified to give expert evidence, if made as a way of conveying relevant facts personally perceived by him, is admissible as evidence of what he perceived.*

(3) *In this section "relevant matter" includes an issue in the proceedings in question."*

This provision is extended to include the evidence of a witness who is not called by s.1 of the Civil Evidence Act 1995, which provides:

"(1) *In civil proceedings evidence shall not be excluded on the ground that it is hearsay.*

(2) *In this Act—*

(a) *hearsay means a statement made otherwise than by a person while giving oral evidence in the proceedings which is tendered as evidence of the matters stated; and*

(b) *references to hearsay include hearsay of whatever degree."*

Section 13 of the 1995 Act provides that a "statement" means "any representation of fact or opinion, however made". Accordingly, as set out in Phipson, at [29-03], this provision "covers statements of opinion admissible under the 1972 Act".

In C v M, it was stated at paragraph 81:

'This issue is addressed in some detail in Phipson, at [33-112], as set out in D (A Child) at [72], which I repeat (with some footnotes incorporated):

"[33-112] Although in general inadmissible, the opinions or beliefs of witnesses who are not experts are admissible in proof of the matters mentioned below, on grounds of necessity, more direct and positive evidence being often unobtainable. Moreover, it has long been thought, and for civil cases it has now been declared by s.3(2) of the Civil Evidence Act 1972, that non-expert opinion may be received as evidence of the facts intended to be conveyed by that expression of opinion. Thus there is no blanket rule that a factual witness may not include opinion evidence in his witness statement in civil cases. There are numerous authorities which exemplify that a witness of fact may give opinion evidence which relates to the factual evidence he is giving, particularly if he has relevant experience or knowledge. An example is where the evidence given is to a hypothetical situation as to what would or could have happened [MAD Atelier International BV v Manes [2021] EWHC 1899 (Comm) at [11]]. In Rasool v West Midlands Passenger Transport Board [[1974] 3 All E.R. 638] an account of a witness of a road accident was received notwithstanding the fact that it contained the words "the bus driver was in no way to blame for the accident". The court treated them as admissible although the 1972 Act did not fall to be considered, and the point was not argued [This passage in the 17th edition of Phipson was followed in Lawrence v Kent County Council [2012] EWCA Civ 493, which observed that time and time again one sees references to the opinions of a factual witness in judgments without any suggestion that they are totally irrelevant (at [25])].

The statute purports to declare the law, and it is thought that the position must be the same in criminal cases. This proposition

> *is given emphatic support by R. v Johnson [[1994] Crim. L.R. 376 CA] where a witness testified that she had seen the victim of a rape and buggery of the defendant shortly after the incident and that although she had initially thought that the victim was play-acting, she had come to believe that her distress was genuine.*
>
> *In civil cases, hearsay evidence of opinion is admissible under s.1 of the Civil Evidence Act 1995 (which renders all hearsay, whether of fact or opinion admissible). This provision extends to admissible non expert opinion of the kind discussed here."*
>
> *I do not propose to quote again from Lawrence v Kent County Council [2012] EWCA Civ 493, which is set out in D (A Child), at [73].'*

The Issues – A Summary

The joint appeal in the Court of Appeal therefore deals with a number of key issues relating to children participation in 1980 Hague Convention cases. It considers the role of solicitors, the role of guardians, how evidence is to be treated and its relevant under the defences of the 1980 Hague Convention. There is likely to be further law by way of further rules cementing some of the points outlined in the guidance.

Inherent Jurisdiction – Role of Children

A useful starting point is the authority of S (A Child) (Abduction: Hearing the Child)[34] and in particular paragraphs 12 – 16 which state:

> *'Proceedings concerning the welfare of a child whether in the Family Court or in the reserved jurisdictions of the High Court are subject to the same fundamental principles concerning effective access to justice for children who are the subjects of the applications that are made. There is no general rule in England and Wales that every child should be a party and that every child be represented by lawyers, by litigation friends or by welfare guardians. In each species of jurisdiction there are rules and practice directions that require or permit different forms of representation depending on the nature of the process and the facts of the case. There is often a delicate balance to be undertaken between the procedural protections that are afforded to a child by the process and the protection that may be necessary in respect of the impact on the child of the process (including the adversarial positions of the child's parents).*
>
> *The underlying concept is that the child must be afforded effective access to justice so that the State does not infringe that child's article 6 and 8 ECHR rights. Without prejudice to the schemes that are in place for public and private law children applications under the Children Act 1989, this case is about the application of the general principles to proceedings in the inherent jurisdiction of the High Court. It should be recollected that in this case A was made a ward of court and was accordingly subject to the prerogative jurisdiction of the Crown otherwise known as the parens patriae jurisdiction, which is administered by the judges of the High Court.*

---

34 [2014] EWCA Civ 1557

There is a dispute between the parties about whether there are general principles that apply in a case of this kind. If there are, the key question that arises is whether the application of those general principles required something to be done that was not done on the facts of this case.

Article 12 of the United Nations Convention on the Rights of the Child 1989 [UNCRC] provides that:

> *"[1] States parties shall assure to the child who is capable of forming his or her own views the right to express those views freely in all matters affecting the child, the views of the child being given due weight in accordance with the age and maturity of the child.*
>
> *[2] For this purpose, the child shall in particular be provided the opportunity to be heard in any judicial and administrative proceedings affecting the child, either directly, or through a representative or an appropriate body, in a manner consistent with the procedural rules of national law."*

The UNCRC creates international obligations rather than domestic rights. That said, it is consistent with and has a persuasive interpretative effect on other international instruments that are binding on the United Kingdom. For example, article 24 of the Charter of Fundamental Rights of the European Union *provides that:*

> *"[1] Children shall have the right to such protection and care as is necessary for their well being. They may express their views freely. Such views shall be taken into consideration on matters which concern them in accordance with their age and maturity.*

> [2] *In all actions relating to children, whether taken by public authorities or private institutions, the child's best interests must be a primary consideration."*

Therefore, in proceedings relating to international abduction, particular under the inherent jurisdiction – there are many ways in which children can participate. However, it is first important to outline what the inherent jurisdiction is. This is because powers and orders within the inherent jurisdiction can be wide-ranging and have far reaching effects, particularly on the children involved. This is because orders such as Passport and Location orders can curtail the free movement of children. Information about their welfare can come under depths of scrutiny.

The Inherent Jurisdiction – General Principles

The key case is Re NY (A Child)[35]. This case outlined the principle that if a party is seeking a return order through the inherent jurisdiction, then the point of reference for the court is the subject child's welfare.

The Supreme court set out 8 principles. These 8 points are what practitioners need to have in mind for any inward or outward abduction case. Each principle will have an impact upon the timetable and therefore must be grappled with urgently. Inward and outward abduction proceedings are 'summary' and therefore an applicant should ensure in particular, that the proceedings are timetabled and each of the below are considered:

> *'55. I respectfully suggest, however, that, before making a summary order under the inherent jurisdiction for this child to be returned to Israel, the Court of Appeal should have given (but*

[35] [2019] UKSC 49

did not give) at least some consideration to eight further, linked, questions.

56. First, the court, which was sitting on 18 June 2019, should have considered whether the evidence before it was sufficiently up to date to enable it then to make the summary order. The mother's statement in answer to the claim under the Convention was dated 29 March 2019. In it she had devoted seven out of 67 paragraphs to assertions of the child's habitual residence in England and of particular circumstances said to demonstrate how happy and settled she had become. In his statement in reply dated 11 April the father had joined issue with the mother's assertions. The oral evidence given by the parties to the judge on 15 April had been limited to the issue of consent to the child's removal from Israel and so had not addressed these matters.

57. Second, the court should have considered whether the judge had made, or whether it could make, findings sufficient to justify the summary order. The only relevant finding made by the judge had been that on 10 January 2019, only seven weeks after her arrival in England, the child had retained habitual residence in Israel. Was that sufficient to justify the making of a summary order five months later? In the light of the policy in favour of the making of substantive welfare determinations by the courts of habitual residence, did there need to be inquiry into the child's habitual residence at the relevant date, which, in the absence of an application, was in this case the date of the proposed order?

58. Third, the court should have considered whether, in order sufficiently to identify what the child's welfare required for the purposes of a summary order, an inquiry should be conducted into any or all of the aspects of welfare specified in section 1(3) of the 1989 Act and, if so, how extensive that inquiry should be: see para 49 above. It might in particular have considered that the third of those aspects, namely "the likely effect on [the child] of any change in [her] circumstances", merited inquiry.

59. Fourth, the court should have considered whether in the light of Practice Direction 12J, an inquiry should be conducted into the disputed allegations made by the mother of domestic abuse and, if so, how extensive that inquiry should be: see para 50 above. The judge had made no findings about them. Instead, in accordance with the E case cited in para 12 above, he had, for the purposes of the claim under the Convention, made a reasonable assumption in relation to the maximum level of risk to the child arising out of any domestic abuse to be perpetrated by the father and had considered that such risk would be contained within acceptable limits by undertakings offered by the father, the enforceability of which in Israel the judge had not explored. Consideration should therefore have been given to whether, in a determination to be governed by the child's welfare, the judge's approach to the mother's allegations remained sufficient.

60. Fifth, the court should have considered whether, without identification in evidence of any arrangements for the child in Israel, in particular of where she and the mother would live, it would be appropriate to conclude that her welfare required her to return there.

61. Sixth, the court should have considered whether, in the light of its consideration of the five matters identified above, any oral evidence should be given by the parties and, if so, upon what aspects and to what extent.

62. Seventh, the court should have considered whether, in the light of its consideration of the same matters, a CAFCASS officer should be directed to prepare a report and, if so, upon what aspects and to what extent. It is noteworthy that in the L case discussed in para 43 above, a CAFCASS report had been

> *prepared. It had been designed to ascertain the boy's wishes and feelings and so was apparently made as if pursuant to section 1(3)(a) of the 1989 Act: see para 14 of Baroness Hale's judgment. In her careful weighing, in paras 34 to 37 of her judgment, of the welfare considerations which militated both in favour of, and against, the boy's return to Texas, Baroness Hale relied to a significant extent upon the content of the CAFCASS report.*
>
> *63. Eighth, the court should have considered whether it needed to compare the relative abilities of the Rabbinical Court in Jerusalem and the Family Court in London to reach a swift resolution of the substantive issues between the parents in relation to the child and to satisfy itself that the Rabbinical Court had power to authorise the mother to relocate with the child back to England: see para 34 above.*
>
> *64. The effect of the above is not to submerge efficient exercise of the inherent jurisdiction to make a summary order within an ocean of onerous judicial obligations. The linked obligations are obligations only to consider the eight specified matters. There is no need for us to contemplate what the proper outcome of the Court of Appeal's consideration of them might have been. It is the fact that it failed even to consider them which yields the conclusion that it conducted no defensible analysis of the child's welfare prior to its determination to make the summary order and which led this court to uphold the mother's appeal'.*

Accordingly, issues relating to PD12J, Cafcass, evidence generally relating to welfare is crucial. How these factors are considered can alter the timetable. If there needs to be a fact-finding, then this will create a delay. A welfare assessment is likely to be ordered only after a fact-finding hearing. Alternatively, if the matter only requires a welfare enquiry, then it should be noted that the paramountcy of the subject child's welfare may not necessarily require a full welfare enquiry. Each case is fact specific. Practitioners should have the 8 principles in consideration always during inherent jurisdiction cases particularly in cases relating to child abduction.

Inward Abduction

It is important practitioners are alive to two possibilities here:

A. The country where the children were abducted is a non-Hague state; or

B. The country where the children were abducted from, is a Hague state, but the inherent jurisdiction needs to be utilised.

In respect of point B, there are circumstances where the 1980 Hague Convention does not apply. For example, if the return is for a child over the aged of 16[36] and therefore the Convention does not apply. In these circumstances, the issue is that of welfare under the inherent jurisdiction. As outlined in Re J (Child Returned Abroad: Convention Rights)[37]

> *'in all non-Convention cases, the courts have consistently held that they must act in accordance with the welfare of the individual child. If they do decide to return the child, that is because it is in his best interests to do so, not because the welfare principle has been superseded by some other consideration'*

Further, Re J makes clear there is a choice before the Court: *'it is plain, therefore, that there is always a choice to be made. Summary return should not be the automatic reaction to any and every unauthorised taking or*

36 Re Q (Children) (1980 Hague Convention: Inherent Jurisdiction Summary Return) [2019] EWHC 490 (Fam) also see Article 4 of the 1980 Hague Convention

37 [2005] 2 FLR 802, at paragraph 25

keeping a child from his home country. On the other hand, summary return may very well be in the best interests of the individual child'[38]

Moreover, as Baroness Hale stated in Re J, the following:

> *'The most one can say, in my view, is that the judge may find it convenient to start from the proposition that it is likely to be better for a child to return to his home country for any disputes about his future to be decided there. A case against his doing so has to be made. But the weight to be given to that proposition will vary enormously from case to case. What may be best for him in the long run may be different from what will be best for him in the short run. It should not be assumed, in this or any other case, that allowing a child to remain here while his future is decided here inevitably means that he will remain here for ever'*[39]

The above is a position. It is not a presumption and therefore depending upon the facts of a case, the issue can be grappled with.

Accordingly, an assessment is that of Children Act 1989 and welfare. In circumstances where there is clearly an international case in existence, there has been a vast amount of case law considering the issue. Therefore, points such as the connection the child has to each competing country[40] the child's views, the legal systems available in each country for example. There will be a broad assessment and in circumstances where a respondent seeks to defend a summary return application, they need to consider having a Cafcass assessment in respect of welfare. Welfare is the

---

38 Paragraph 28

39 Paragraph 32

40 Re L (Minors) (Wardship: Jurisdiction) [1974] 1 WLR 250

key concept and as described by Lord Donaldson MR in Re F (Minor) (Abduction: Jurisdiction)[41]:

> *'The welfare of the child is indeed the paramount consideration, but it has to be considered in two different contexts. The first is the context of which court shall decide what the child's best interests require. The second context, which only arises if it has first been decided that the welfare of the child requires that the English rather than a foreign court shall decide what are the requirements of the child, is what orders as to custody, care and control and so on, should be made.'*

Equally, in respect of any points relating to the legal system, there should be a consideration of a Part25 expert to address the issue. The case of LM v DR[42] demonstrates the issue. The party resisting a summary return will have to demonstrate that the issue of the legal system in that country is relevant to the welfare of the child in circumstances where a return order is resisted.

Another consideration is the voice of the child. Just like 1980 Hague Convention cases, there is a vast number of reported decisions on the issue. Afterall, when the issue is that of welfare, the child's views are going to be a consideration within the checklist of factors and could ultimately, be a key one at that Practitioners should address this at the first case management hearing. Cafcass should be contacted in order to obtain their timescales to do a report as well as the remit of the report. As outlined earlier, a full welfare assessment may not be necessary and therefore the timing for the report to be completed may differ. The scope of the report should be addresses at the first hearing and recorded clearly in the report.

---

41 [1991] 1 FLR 1

42 [2016] EWHC 1943 (Fam)

In terms of the essential nature of the child's voice, the Court of Appeal in Re S (A Child)[43] outlines the following international obligations:

> '[15] Article 12 of the United Nations Convention on the Rights of the Child 1989 [UNCRC] provides that:
>
> > '1. *States parties shall assure to the child who is capable of forming his or her own views the right to express those views freely in all matters affecting the child, the views of the child being given due weight in accordance with the age and maturity of the child.*
> >
> > 2. *For this purpose, the child shall in particular be provided the opportunity to be heard in any judicial and administrative proceedings affecting the child, either directly, or through a representative or an appropriate body, in a manner consistent with the procedural rules of national law."*
>
> *[16] The UNCRC creates international obligations rather than domestic rights. That said, it is consistent with and has a persuasive interpretative effect on other international instruments that are binding on the United Kingdom. For example, art 24 of the Charter of Fundamental Rights of the European Union provides that:*
>
> > "1. *Children shall have the right to such protection and care as is necessary for their well being. They may express their views freely. Such views shall be taken into consideration on matters which concern them in accordance with their age and maturity.*

43 (Abduction: Hearing the Child) [2014] EWCA Civ 1557

> 2. *In all actions relating to children, whether taken by public authorities or private institutions, the child's best interests must be a primary consideration.'*

The 1980 Hague Convention would also not apply if the applicant cannot prove rights of custody immediately prior to the retention nor removal pursuant to Article 3[44].

Outward Abduction

Proceedings relating to outward abductions tend to be more difficult to progress and timetable and require practitioners to think strategically from the outset of proceedings. This is because, in circumstances where a respondent has abducted a child to a non-Hague state, then a number of practical obstacles arise and can materialise. Firstly, the action of the respondent to take a child to a non-Hague state within itself is a problem. The non-Hague state has no bilateral agreement with the Courts of England and Wales and therefore the respondent may be seeking to evade justice. Other issues that often arise in this case, which can involve children are:

A. Whether to go without notice or not;

B. Any assistance that can be obtained from agencies / government bodies;

C. Tracing and locating the respondent / child;

D. Ensuring the respondent engages with the proceedings;

E. Enabling the child's voice to be heard; and

[44] Re W (Abduction: Father's Rights) [998] 2 FLR 146

F. Ensuring compliance.

Tracing and locating the respondent / child

It is a sad reality that a respondent could abduct children to a non-Hague state they either are from, or to where they have no existing links. It can be difficult to locate a respondent in the first place. Nonetheless, upon Tipstaff orders being made, Tipstaff can undertake an international movement check. This will outline the date and time the children and respondent travelled and to where to. Once this is located, then requests can be made to the country for assistance in providing information. Of course, there may be nothing stopping the respondent from leaving one country to another and then this is where the difficulty materialises.

Alternatively, disclosure orders against bank accounts and phone record companies may be able to help in finding where the respondent is. Additionally, attendance orders against close family members of the respondent (who are still in England) for them to attend the High Court and give evidence on oath about any information they know is also an option.

Tipstaff Orders

One matter that is unique to inherent jurisdiction proceedings in the ability to obtain Tipstaff orders. There are many different reasons for why a Tipstaff order may be sought. Typically, these are only sought by applicant to proceedings, the local authority in public law proceedings or proceedings relating to the protection of children, such as when a local authority is seeking a Forced Marriage Protection Order or Female Genital Mutilation Order.

Before considering applying for a Tipstaff orders, practitioners must contact Tipstaff before seeking any order from the High Court relating to Tipstaff orders. The Tipstaff possess the ultimate experience in all matters relating to abduction and other risks associated with matters in the High Court. Their advice is necessary and they have their own forms to complete and often the judge will check with Tipstaff as to their views on the orders sought.

If any Tipstaff orders are made at court, they will be drafted by the Court Associate and not the practitioner. The precedent orders are available to enable practitioners to consider the terms and implications of such orders, however they are always drafted by the associate.

As a point of first reference, practitioners should consider the FPR, PD12D, Rule 7.1 – 7.4. These rules briefly set out the role of Tipstaff:

> '*7.1*
>
> *The tipstaff is the enforcement officer for all orders made in the High Court. The tipstaff's jurisdiction extends throughout England and Wales. Every applicable order made in the High Court is addressed to the tipstaff in children and family matters (eg 'The Court hereby directs the Tipstaff of the High Court of Justice, whether acting by himself or his assistants or a police officer as follows…').*
>
> *7.2*
>
> *The tipstaff may effect an arrest and then inform the police. Sometimes the local bailiff or police will detain a person in custody until the tipstaff arrives to collect that person or give further directions as to the disposal of the matter. The tipstaff may also make a forced entry although there will generally be a uniformed police officer standing by to make sure there is no breach of the peace.*

7.3

There is only one tipstaff (with two assistants) but the tipstaff can also call on any constable or bailiff to assist in carrying out the tipstaff's duties.

7.4

The majority of the tipstaff's work involves locating children and taking them into protective custody, including cases of child abduction abroad'

Passport Orders

If the applicant has set out in the witness statement that there is a risk the respondent may seek to evade participating in any court proceedings or may be a flight risk to another country, then a passport order may be necessary. A passport order includes various prohibitions with a penal notice attached to it (in the event the respondent breaches any order, an application for committal can be made). A passport order is addressed to the respondent who must hand over any travel document (such as a passport, ID cards) to the Tipstaff and the respondent will be prohibited from seeking to obtain or apply for further travel documents. Equally, the passport order will include prohibitions to ensure that the respondent and children must not leave the jurisdiction and a port alert is created. The port alert will flag up any attempt of a person leaving the jurisdiction or entering the jurisdiction. If any third party stands in the way of compliance with a passport order, then the police also have powers over them as well. For example, if Tipstaff seeks to execute a passport order at a property but a non-subject party is evasive and making it difficult for Tipstaff to execute the order, then they themselves can get into trouble.

Mr Justice Cobb in Re P (Discharge of Passport Order)[45] provided useful guidance in respect of passport orders. Practitioners on both sides of the coin, those seeking a passport order or those seeking a discharge of passport order should refer to this authority. His lordship stated after reviewing the relevant authorities:

> *'Tipstaff passport order is a useful tool in the judicial armoury, particularly in circumstances where:*
>
> *(i) a court needs to take urgent action to try to prevent a parent from removing a child out of the country (see Wilson J as he then was in B v B (Injunction: Restraint on Leaving Jurisdiction) [1997] 2 FLR 148 remarked at p.153: 'B v B [1997]');*
>
> *(ii) where there is an assessed risk that a foreign parent may misuse a period of contact in England in order to remove a child overseas (again, B v B [1997] at p.153);*
>
> *(iii) where (as here) the court wishes to ensure the attendance of a person at a court hearing within the jurisdiction, and there is a risk that, absent such an order, the person may flee the country before doing so (see for instance Thorpe J as he then was in Re S (Financial Provision: Non-Resident) [1996] 1 FCR 148); and (iv) where without such an order the execution of an interlocutory order may be stymied (B v B [1997] at p.154).*
> *32. But a passport order is a potent order, with significant implications, whose use it seems to me should be tightly controlled; thus:*
>
> *i) A passport order should only ever be made for a finite period of time (this is likely to be, as it was in this case, for a period of six months before it would have expired*

45 [2020] EWHC 3009 (Fam), at paragraphs 31 – 40

unexecuted) (see Re L (A Child), Re Oddin **[2016] EWCA Civ 173***);*

ii) A passport order should not be made where the sole purpose is to coerce the respondent into action of a particular kind; in his submissions, the father rightly referenced in this regard Hobhouse LJ's judgment in B v B [1994] 2 FLR 479 at 486 and Sir James Munby P in Re B (A Child: Evidence: Passport Order) [2014] EWCA Civ 843, *[2015] 1 FCR 75, [2015] 1 FLR 871 at [33]'*

Practitioners must ensure that they have the exact spelling of the respondent's name and the children's names to ensure the port alerts can be registered as appropriate and the children/respondent do not leave the jurisdiction. Practitioners must ensure that they take instructions from the applicant in respect of all possible travel documents/passports the respondent and children may have. This is because when the passport order is executed, the relevant documents can be sought and seized. At court, the barrister or solicitor must complete the Tipstaff forms and include all relevant information. Upon the order being made by the judge, the Court Associate will have regard to the forms and compile the Tipstaff order. If there is a spelling mistake in the names or dates of birth, then the port alert might not be flagged up and triggered. Therefore, in cases where abduction is sought to be prevented, if there is a spelling mistake in existence, abduction might happen. It is crucial that practitioners check all Tipstaff orders for errors before they are executed.

A port alert is a useful tool that is contained within Tipstaff orders such as a passport order. If a party is seeking a port alert, then as Mostyn J indicated in A v B (Port Alert)[46] at paragraph 42 outlined: '*the initial application for a port alert order will almost invariably be made ex parte for obvious reasons*'. Practitioners should however note in the decision of A v B, Mostyn J did highlight the procedure for port alerts to be made in the

[46] [2021] EWHC 1716 (Fam)

local family court as opposed to the High Court. There are differences to the procedure and purpose. Mostyn J outlined the following process and reasoning as paragraphs 37 to 40 of his judgment:

> '*In my judgment, therefore, the Family Court plainly does have the power to issue a freestanding port alert order, where such an order is justified on the facts and is an incidental and supplemental order to give effect to a decision of the Family Court.*
>
> *The most obvious example is the situation where the Family Court has made a prohibited steps order preventing parents from taking a child out of the country without the other's consent or a court order. A port alert in such circumstances is simply acting as a supplemental safety net to ensure the efficacy of the prohibited steps order. It would be highly anomalous if the Family Court had power to issue a bench warrant to bring a parent who had gone on the run with the children before the court but did not have the power to issue a port alert order to prevent the children leaving the country.*
>
> *I would not expect freestanding port alert orders to be made by the Family Court routinely. Such an order should only be made where the applicant demonstrates with clear evidence that there is a real and imminent risk that the children in question will be removed from England and Wales. When assessing that risk the court will not demand proof that it is more likely than not that the children will be removed; it will, nonetheless, still expect proof of a degree of probability not far short of that standard. It is important that applications for these orders are not made in reliance on evidence which amounts to no more than mere assertion or which is otherwise flimsy or unsubstantiated.*
>
> *When such an order is made the default position should be that it lasts for only 28 days in the first instance and that any extension of that period should only be ordered on a subsequent*

> *inter partes hearing. In my opinion this is a key provision which needs to be adhered to strictly'*

Therefore, there is a difference relating to a prohibited steps order and a port alert. For the purposes of this book, what practitioners need to know is that if proceedings are in the High Court and the inherent jurisdiction is being utilised, Tipstaff will be responsible (if a order is made) for enacting a port alert which are contained within their orders. Notwithstanding this, practitioners must be on high alert. Given there is the power for the Family Court to make a freestanding port alert, practitioners can be expected to explain as to why a Tipstaff order is preferred and necessary. There may be a number of reasons for this For example, it could be submitted that the proceedings will need to remain in the High Court in any event for a number of complex reasons or due to the fact that a port alert by Tipstaff is enacted fairly fast, often on the same day and further, Tipstaff orders enables Tipstaff to do an international movement trace to ascertain whether the respondent and children have left England and Wales, and if so when and how which might be important evidence relating to the case or strategy to be adopted

Location Order

A location order is often sought at the first hearing with disclosure orders. The purpose of a location order is to locate the relevant children and respondent. It includes all the similar provisions that appear in the passport order in respect of the prohibitions and port alert. However, a location order once served on someone must inform the Tipstaff of the whereabouts of the subject children or any known information to assist the Tipstaff in locating the children. A location order often works in tandem with a disclosure order. For example, once a disclosure order reveals the last known address of the respondent then this information is provided by the solicitor for the applicant to Tipstaff who will then seek to execute the order.

Collection Orders

A collection order will contain all the provisions of a passport order, in the sense that a port alert will be enacted, and the passports of the respondents will be seized and held by Tipstaff if found. However, a collection order has a very specific purpose. It is an order requiring Tipstaff to collect and return a child or place the child with someone else. For example, in public law proceedings a Local Authority may not be able to find a subject child or a child in their care may have vanished and is with a parent or someone else. A collection order will enable the subject child to be placed back to the care and control of the Local Authority. Or alternatively, in private law proceedings there may be a Child Arrangements Order for a child to live with a specific parent. The other parent may not be happy with this outcome or may breach this order. In these circumstances, a collection order can be sought to ensure the child is returned to the named individual, such as a parent.

One point to emphasise about a collection order is that it is a Tipstaff order. In the private law context, practitioners should consider whether a recovery order is more suitable. This equally applies to a Local Authority in public law proceedings. A recovery order can be made by a family law judge in the context of public or private law proceedings. The order will specify that a named police force are to recover the child and place the child in the applicant's care (such as a parent in private law proceedings, or a local authority in public law proceedings). In contrast, within inherent jurisdiction High Court proceedings, a collection order may be particularly attractive in circumstances where it is believed that there may be real risk to the subject child, by means of harm, abduction or if the child has become difficult to locate by means of absconding a placement.

Tipstaff Orders being executed

A Tipstaff order being executed has two forms of impact. Firstly, the respondent will be alerted to the fact there are now court proceedings in existence (albeit Tipstaff will not serve the court documentation on them) and has their own and the children's travel documents seized and informed about the other prohibitions as contained within the Tipstaff order. Upon this happening, the solicitors for the applicant must arrange for personal service of the documents to be served on the respondent so that they are aware of what has happened and to be informed about the next court date. Secondly, the respondent no longer has the travel documents of their own or the children's travel documents in their possession. These are instead held by Tipstaff either until the conclusion of the court proceedings or further order of the court. The issue in respect of Tipstaff orders must be considered at each and every hearing, and Tipstaff will provide the standard wording that needs to be included in the order in the event that an existing Tipstaff order is extended, varied or discharged.

Once an order has been made, it is likely the order will continue until they are executed. For example, if the respondent and children cannot be found then the order will be extended at each without notice hearing. In terms of the law about continuation of Tipstaff orders, practitioners should note the comments of the Court of Appeal in *Re K (Forced Marriage: Passport Order)*[47]

> '*... an open-ended passport order or travel ban should only be imposed in the most exceptional of cases and where the court can look sufficiently far into the future to be satisfied that highly restrictive orders of that nature will be required indefinitely. In all other cases, the court should impose a time limit when making such orders. The time limit will vary from case-to-case and, like all other elements, be a bespoke provision imposing a*

47 [2020] EWCA Civ 19, at para 67

> *restriction only in so far as that is justified on the facts as found. Unless the court can see with clarity that there will be no need for any continuing order after a particular date, for example when it is clear that the circumstances will change so that the risk is removed, the appropriate course will be for the court to list the matter for further review a short time before the passport and/or travel ban will otherwise expire'*

And[48]:

> *'A travel ban and a Passport Order are highly intrusive in terms of their impact upon the private life and freedom of movement of the individual concerned'*

Cobb J in Re P[49] further stated:

> *'Furthermore, once granted and passports are seized:-*
>
> *iii) The passport order is unlikely to endure beyond the conclusion of the proceedings in which the order is made (Re M (Children) (Care Proceedings: Passport Orders)* [2017] EWCA Civ 69*). If an order for a passport to be held indefinitely can ever be justified (i.e. after the conclusion of proceedings), it is likely only to be in an unusual and probably quite extreme case where it can be demonstrated, after a close evaluation of the degree of risk to the children and of the harm to which they will be exposed if the risk becomes a reality, that such a serious invasion of the passport-holder's rights is proportionate and necessary: Re M (above); cf, Re A (A Child)* [2016] EWCA Civ 572, *[2016] 4 WLR 111, paras 69-70;*

---

48 Ibid, at para 77

49 [2020] EWHC 3009 (Fam), at para 32

> *iv) Consistent with the principles above, and the observations from the authorities, it seems to me to be incumbent on the court to keep under careful review during ongoing proceedings the need to deprive a person of their passport, under a tipstaff passport order; such an order should not remain in place for any longer than is necessary to achieve the legitimate desired protection or outcome.*
>
> *The removal of an individual's passport, even on a temporary basis, be that of an adult or child, is a very significant incursion into the individual's freedom and personal autonomy. It is never an order that can be made lightly (Hayden J in London Borough of Tower Hamlets v M* [2015] EWHC 869*); a passport order should in my judgment rarely if ever be more than a very temporary measure'.*

Participation of Children – Difference between Wardship and Inherent Jurisdiction

As the above highlights, the inherent jurisdiction is extremely wide ranging. Children can be abducted, they can be subject to Tipstaff orders and have their rights to travel curtailed. Ultimately therefore, the voice of the child in proceedings is a significant one.

In the inherent jurisdiction proceedings, it is more common that children can be made a ward of a court. This is different to the inherent jurisdiction and must not be confused with one another.

An interesting feature of High Court proceedings is the difference between the inherent jurisdiction and wardship. Both areas are dealt with in the High Court, but whilst they are at times linked, they must be separated as otherwise practitioners fall into a trap of seeking certain relief that is not necessary. It is a common misconception that the subject children have to be made wards in order for the court to exercise its inherent jurisdiction. This is not the case. The Family Procedure Rules

['FPR'] helpfully distil this myth and they distinguish the different characteristics of wardship. For example, the FPR 2010[50] defines[51] the distinguishing characteristics of wardship as follows:

> '(a) *custody of a child who is a ward is vested in the court; and*
>
> (b) *although day to day care and control of the ward is given to an individual or to a local authority, no important step can be taken in the child's life without the court's consent*'.

In terms of a case law example, Parker J in AB v CD[52] stated the following:

> '*Wardship is a way in which the 'inherent jurisdiction with regard to children' (ie the parens patriae jurisdiction) may be exercised. Once a child is a ward of court, that child is under the continuous protection of the court, even after a final order has been made determining the issues in respect of that child. Once a child is ward of court that child's place or country of residence or school cannot be changed without a court order*'.

Participation of Children – Inherent Jurisdiction & Welfare

As the above highlights, there can be occasions where a child is a ward of the court. But equally, there can be occasions where they are subject, or party to proceedings involving just the inherent jurisdiction.

In consequence of Re NY above, there is a wide variety of ways children can participate. Similarities exist with private law children disputes, save for the facts in international child abduction proceedings can be much

50 Practice Direction 12D, para 1.3

51 Ibid, para 1.3 (a) and (b)

52 [2014] 1 FLR 1439, para 51

more grave. For example, the child may be abducted in another state, or not even found. Cafcass have a useful role to play. In the High Court, same with 1980 Hague Convention cases, there is a specific High Court Cafcass Team that deals with international proceedings.

Cafcass can be tasked to do reports. The reports are not limited like 1980 Hague Convention, because under the inherent jurisdiction the 'best interests' of the child is the courts paramount consideration. Therefore, reports can be full welfare reports, or limited wishes and feelings reports. There can be numerous reports during the course of the proceedings and Cafcass will be tasked with advising about separate representation.

In child abduction disputes, particularly where children are abducted or prevented from returning to England and Wales, the facts can be so concerning that it is normally in the interests of the child to have a guardian acting for them. This provides the Court with a lot of assistance when it comes to timetabling proceedings and dealing with complicated international issues that can arise. At times, a child may even be added as a party to proceedings even where the child cannot make contact with the Cafcass officer. This is because the Cafcass officers duty is to the court, and an appointment of a solicitor will arise and as such, whenever the court is considering orders under the inherent jurisdiction, the submissions on behalf of the guardian will be a key consideration

Children As a Party – Inherent Jurisdiction Disputes

In private disputes between parents in the High Court, if the inherent jurisdiction is being utilised then practitioners must have regard to the trajectory of the case. In the sense, what is the ultimate goal of the proceedings? If the inherent jurisdiction is being utilised for particular purposes, eventually a final order may need to be made. As outlined earlier in this chapter, a fact-finding hearing may be necessary. Also, practitioners must also consider having children joined to proceedings if required. It can be assumed in circumstances where proceedings are remaining in the High Court there is an element of complexity in existence. Notwithstanding this, the test and approach is within the Family Procedure Rules.

To start with, PD16A, 7.1 outlines:

> "*Making the child a party to the proceedings is a step that will be taken only in cases which involve an issue of significant difficulty and consequently will occur in only a minority of cases. Before taking the decision to make the child a party, consideration should be given to whether an alternative route might be preferable, such as asking an officer of the Service or a Welsh family proceedings officer to carry out further work or by making a referral to social services or, possibly, by obtaining expert evidence*".

Therefore, we have considered earlier in this chapter the 1980 Hague Convention. The rules are different, as is the practice in inherent jurisdiction proceedings when it comes to children being joined to the proceedings. As previously outlined, facts in inherent jurisdiction proceedings can be rather extreme because a children may be abducted, not found or in a jurisdiction they no longer wish to be in. Further, a carer of the child may be stranded in another state and therefore there is separation in existence. All of these welfare issues are further complicated by the fact of the international nature of the proceedings.

In terms of the test to be applied when this issue arises, practitioners should consider the checklist at PD16A, 7.2:

> '*7.2*
>
> *The decision to make the child a party will always be exclusively that of the court, made in the light of the facts and circumstances of the particular case. The following are offered, solely by way of guidance, as circumstances which may justify the making of such an order –*

(a) *where an officer of the Service or Welsh family proceedings officer has notified the court that in the opinion of that officer the child should be made a party;*

(b) *where the child has a standpoint or interest which is inconsistent with or incapable of being represented by any of the adult parties;*

(c) *where there is an intractable dispute over residence or contact, including where all contact has ceased, or where there is irrational but implacable hostility to contact or where the child may be suffering harm associated with the contact dispute;*

(d) *where the views and wishes of the child cannot be adequately met by a report to the court;*

(e) *where an older child is opposing a proposed course of action;*

(f) *where there are complex medical or mental health issues to be determined or there are other unusually complex issues that necessitate separate representation of the child;*

(g) *where there are international complications outside child abduction, in particular where it may be necessary for there to be discussions with overseas authorities or a foreign court;*

(h) *where there are serious allegations of physical, sexual or other abuse in relation to the child or there are allegations of domestic violence not capable of being resolved with the help of an officer of the Service or Welsh family proceedings officer;*

(i) *where the proceedings concern more than one child and the welfare of the children is in conflict or one child is in a particularly disadvantaged position;*

(j) *where there is a contested issue about scientific testing'*

Points (b), (c), (g) and (h) are common features that can arise in High Court private disputes arising out of proceedings where the inherent jurisdiction has or continues to be exercised. In such circumstances it is very likely the question of appointing a guardian will be an early consideration. This is another mechanism in which children can play a key role in participating in proceedings.

Conclusion of Chapter

As this chapter has outlined, the role and participation of children in international disputes is wide-ranging, reflecting the seriousness of the issues that often arise, which are also complicated and international in nature. The guardian plays a very useful role in advancing a child's wishes, or defence where applicability, but also – the benefit of a High Court Cafcass Team is that the officers are familiar with international disputes, as this is what they are tasked with on a daily basis.

MORE BOOKS BY
LAW BRIEF PUBLISHING

A selection of our other titles available now:-

'A Practical Guide to the Independent School Standards – September 2023 Edition' by Sarah McKimm
'A Practical Guide to Estate Administration and Crypto Assets' by Richard Marshall
'A Practical Guide to Managing GDPR Data Subject Access Requests – Second Edition' by Patrick O'Kane
'A Practical Guide to Parental Alienation in Private and Public Law Children Cases' by Sam King QC & Frankie Shama
'Contested Heritage – Removing Art from Land and Historic Buildings' by Richard Harwood QC, Catherine Dobson, David Sawtell
'The Limits of Separate Legal Personality: When Those Running a Company Can Be Held Personally Liable for Losses Caused to Third Parties Outside of the Company' by Dr Mike Wilkinson
'A Practical Guide to Transgender Law' by Robin Moira White & Nicola Newbegin
'A Practical Guide to 'Stranded Spouses' in Family Law' by Mani Singh Basi
'A Practical Guide to Residential Freehold Conveyancing' by Lorraine Richardson
'A Practical Guide to Pensions on Divorce for Lawyers' by Bryan Scant
'A Practical Guide to Challenging Sham Marriage Allegations in Immigration Law' by Priya Solanki
'A Practical Guide to Digital Communications Evidence in Criminal Law' by Sam Willis
'A Practical Guide to Legal Rights in Scotland' by Sarah-Jane Macdonald
'A Practical Guide to New Build Conveyancing' by Paul Sams & Rebecca East
'A Practical Guide to Defending Barristers in Disciplinary Cases' by Marc Beaumont
'A Practical Guide to Inherited Wealth on Divorce' by Hayley Trim
'A Practical Guide to Practice Direction 12J and Domestic Abuse in Private Law Children Proceedings' by Rebecca Cross & Malvika Jaganmohan

'A Practical Guide to Confiscation and Restraint' by Narita Bahra QC, John Carl Townsend, David Winch
'A Practical Guide to the Law of Forests in Scotland' by Philip Buchan
'A Practical Guide to Health and Medical Cases in Immigration Law' by Rebecca Chapman & Miranda Butler
'A Practical Guide to Bad Character Evidence for Criminal Practitioners by Aparna Rao
'A Practical Guide to Extradition Law post-Brexit' by Myles Grandison et al
'A Practical Guide to Hoarding and Mental Health for Housing Lawyers' by Rachel Coyle
'A Practical Guide to Psychiatric Claims in Personal Injury – 2nd Edition' by Liam Ryan
'Stephens on Contractual Indemnities' by Richard Stephens
'A Practical Guide to the EU Succession Regulation' by Richard Frimston
'A Practical Guide to Solicitor and Client Costs – 2nd Edition' by Robin Dunne
'Constructive Dismissal – Practice Pointers and Principles' by Benjimin Burgher
'A Practical Guide to Religion and Belief Discrimination Claims in the Workplace' by Kashif Ali
'A Practical Guide to the Law of Medical Treatment Decisions' by Ben Troke
'Fundamental Dishonesty and QOCS in Personal Injury Proceedings: Law and Practice' by Jake Rowley
'A Practical Guide to the Law in Relation to School Exclusions' by Charlotte Hadfield & Alice de Coverley
'A Practical Guide to Divorce for the Silver Separators' by Karin Walker
'The Right to be Forgotten – The Law and Practical Issues' by Melissa Stock
'A Practical Guide to Planning Law and Rights of Way in National Parks, the Broads and AONBs' by James Maurici QC, James Neill et al
'A Practical Guide to Election Law' by Tom Tabori
'A Practical Guide to the Law in Relation to Surrogacy' by Andrew Powell
'A Practical Guide to Claims Arising from Fatal Accidents – 2nd Edition' by James Patience
'A Practical Guide to the Ownership of Employee Inventions – From Entitlement to Compensation' by James Tumbridge & Ashley Roughton
'A Practical Guide to Asbestos Claims' by Jonathan Owen & Gareth McAloon

'A Practical Guide to Stamp Duty Land Tax in England and Northern Ireland' by Suzanne O'Hara

'A Practical Guide to the Law of Farming Partnerships' by Philip Whitcomb

'Covid-19, Homeworking and the Law – The Essential Guide to Employment and GDPR Issues' by Forbes Solicitors

'Covid-19 and Criminal Law – The Essential Guide' by Ramya Nagesh

'Covid-19 and Family Law in England and Wales – The Essential Guide' by Safda Mahmood

'A Practical Guide to the Law of Unlawful Eviction and Harassment – 2nd Edition' by Stephanie Lovegrove

'Covid-19, Brexit and the Law of Commercial Leases – The Essential Guide' by Mark Shelton

'A Practical Guide to Costs in Personal Injury Claims – 2nd Edition' by Matthew Hoe

'A Practical Guide to the General Data Protection Regulation (GDPR) – 2nd Edition' by Keith Markham

'Ellis on Credit Hire – Sixth Edition' by Aidan Ellis & Tim Kevan

'A Practical Guide to Working with Litigants in Person and McKenzie Friends in Family Cases' by Stuart Barlow

'Protecting Unregistered Brands: A Practical Guide to the Law of Passing Off' by Lorna Brazell

'A Practical Guide to Secondary Liability and Joint Enterprise Post-Jogee' by Joanne Cecil & James Mehigan

'A Practical Guide to the Pre-Action RTA Claims Protocol for Personal Injury Lawyers' by Antonia Ford

'A Practical Guide to Neighbour Disputes and the Law' by Alexander Walsh

'A Practical Guide to Forfeiture of Leases' by Mark Shelton

'A Practical Guide to Coercive Control for Legal Practitioners and Victims' by Rachel Horman

'A Practical Guide to the Law of Driverless Cars – Second Edition' by Alex Glassbrook, Emma Northey & Scarlett Milligan

'A Practical Guide to TOLATA Claims' by Greg Williams

'A Practical Guide to Elderly Law – 2nd Edition' by Justin Patten

'A Practical Guide to Responding to Housing Disrepair and Unfitness Claims' by Iain Wightwick

‘A Practical Guide to the Law of Bullying and Harassment in the Workplace’ by Philip Hyland
‘How to Be a Freelance Solicitor: A Practical Guide to the SRA-Regulated Freelance Solicitor Model’ by Paul Bennett
‘A Practical Guide to Prison Injury Claims’ by Malcolm Johnson
‘A Practical Guide to the Small Claims Track – 2nd Edition’ by Dominic Bright
‘A Practical Guide to Advising Clients at the Police Station’ by Colin Stephen McKeown-Beaumont
‘A Practical Guide to Antisocial Behaviour Injunctions’ by Iain Wightwick
‘Practical Mediation: A Guide for Mediators, Advocates, Advisers, Lawyers, and Students in Civil, Commercial, Business, Property, Workplace, and Employment Cases’ by Jonathan Dingle with John Sephton
‘The Mini-Pupillage Workbook’ by David Boyle
‘A Practical Guide to Crofting Law’ by Brian Inkster
‘A Practical Guide to the Law of Domain Names and Cybersquatting’ by Andrew Clemson
‘A Practical Guide to the Law of Gender Pay Gap Reporting’ by Harini Iyengar
‘NHS Whistleblowing and the Law’ by Joseph England
‘Employment Law and the Gig Economy’ by Nigel Mackay & Annie Powell
‘A Practical Guide to Noise Induced Hearing Loss (NIHL) Claims’ by Andrew Mckie, Ian Skeate, Gareth McAloon
‘An Introduction to Beauty Negligence Claims – A Practical Guide for the Personal Injury Practitioner’ by Greg Almond
‘Intercompany Agreements for Transfer Pricing Compliance’ by Paul Sutton
‘Zen and the Art of Mediation’ by Martin Plowman
‘A Practical Guide to the SRA Principles, Individual and Law Firm Codes of Conduct 2019 – What Every Law Firm Needs to Know’ by Paul Bennett
‘A Practical Guide to Adoption for Family Lawyers’ by Graham Pegg
‘A Practical Guide to Industrial Disease Claims’ by Andrew Mckie & Ian Skeate
‘A Practical Guide to Conducting a Sheriff Court Proof’ by Andrew Stevenson
‘A Practical Guide to Vicarious Liability’ by Mariel Irvine
‘A Practical Guide to Applications for Landlord’s Consent and Variation of Leases’ by Mark Shelton
‘A Practical Guide to Relief from Sanctions Post-Mitchell and Denton’ by Peter Causton

'A Practical Guide to Equity Release for Advisors' by Paul Sams
'A Practical Guide to Financial Services Claims' by Chris Hegarty
'The Law of Houses in Multiple Occupation: A Practical Guide to HMO Proceedings' by Julian Hunt
'Occupiers, Highways and Defective Premises Claims: A Practical Guide Post-Jackson – 2nd Edition' by Andrew Mckie
'A Practical Guide to Financial Ombudsman Service Claims' by Adam Temple & Robert Scrivenor
'A Practical Guide to Running Housing Disrepair and Cavity Wall Claims: 2nd Edition' by Andrew Mckie & Ian Skeate
'A Practical Guide to Holiday Sickness Claims – 2nd Edition' by Andrew Mckie & Ian Skeate
'Arguments and Tactics for Personal Injury and Clinical Negligence Claims' by Dorian Williams
'A Practical Guide to Drone Law' by Rufus Ballaster, Andrew Firman, Eleanor Clot
'A Practical Guide to Compliance for Personal Injury Firms Working With Claims Management Companies' by Paul Bennett
'RTA Allegations of Fraud in a Post-Jackson Era: The Handbook – 2nd Edition' by Andrew Mckie
'RTA Personal Injury Claims: A Practical Guide Post-Jackson' by Andrew Mckie
'On Experts: CPR35 for Lawyers and Experts' by David Boyle
'An Introduction to Personal Injury Law' by David Boyle

www.ingramcontent.com/pod-product-compliance
Lightning Source LLC
LaVergne TN
LVHW022101200926
848481LV00003B/1020